Meeting
Standards
Through
Integrated
Curriculum

Susan M. Drake
Rebecca C. Burns

Association for Supervision and Curriculum Development
Alexandria, Virginia USA

Association for Supervision and Curriculum Development
1703 N. Beauregard St. • Alexandria, VA 22311-1714 USA
Telephone: 800-933-2723 or 703-578-9600 • Fax: 703-575-5400
Web site: http://www.ascd.org • E-mail: member@ascd.org

Gene R. Carter, *Executive Director;* Nancy Modrak, *Director of Publishing;* Julie Houtz, *Director of Book Editing &*
Production; Ernesto Yermoli, *Project Manager;* Reece Quiñones, *Senior Graphic Designer;* Keith Demmons, *Desktop*
Publishing Specialist; Tracey Smith, *Production Manager.*

Printed in the United States of America. Cover art copyright © 2004 by ASCD.

ASCD publications present a variety of viewpoints. The views expressed or implied in this book should not be inter-
preted as official positions of the Association.

All Web links in this book are correct as of the publication date below but may have become inactive or otherwise modified since that time. If you notice a deactivated or changed link, please e-mail books@ascd.org with the words "Link
Update" in the subject line. In your message, please specify the Web link, the book title, and the page number on which
the link appears.

Paperback ISBN: 0-87120-840-7 • ASCD product #103011 • List Price: $24.95 ($19.95 ASCD member price, direct from
ASCD only)
e-books ($24.95): netLibrary ISBN 0-87120-955-1 • ebrary 0-87120-956-X   s2/04

Library of Congress Cataloging-in-Publication Data

Drake, Susan M., 1944-
  Meeting standards through integrated curriculum / Susan Drake and Rebecca Burns.
     p. cm.
  Includes bibliographical references and index.
  ISBN 0-87120-840-7 (alk. paper)
  1. Education--Curricula--United States. 2. Interdisciplinary approach in education--United States. 3. Education--
Standards--United States. I. Burns, Rebecca Crawford. II. Title.
  LB1570.D697 2004
  375'.00973--dc22
                                         2003026668

10 09 08 07 06 05 04   12 11 10 9 8 7 6 5 4 3 2 1

Meeting Standards Through Integrated Curriculum

Acknowledgments

Our heartfelt thanks to:

The educators who shared their experiences in this book and who gave so generously of their time and wisdom.

Linda Santrock for her excellent work pulling the manuscript together.

Joanne Reid for her incisive editing.

Sonja Upton, Ellie Phillips, and Melissa Rubocki for their tireless hours of exploration into the processes of integrating the curriculum—and for sharing in a rich dialogue.

Adrian DeTullio for asking somewhat skeptically how one could integrate the curriculum and still cover the standards, then having the courage to seek the answer—and Debra Attenborough for helping in this task.

Michael Manley-Casimir, Tony Giblin, and Adele Thomas for their helpful suggestions.

Nancy Modrak, Julie Houtz, and Scott Willis at ASCD for nurturing the book to life, and Ernesto Yermoli and Kathleen Florio for their expert editing.

Introduction

How can we ensure maximum student achievement?

How can we be sure that there is truly no child left behind?

How can evaluation procedures inform us that the students are learning what we want them to learn?

How do we compare with other schools, jurisdictions, states/provinces, and countries?

How can we ensure that teachers are teaching what they are supposed to be teaching?

These questions dominate educational conversations in the 21st century. Educators are working in an era of accountability. They must show evidence that the students under their care are achieving in ways that ultimately lead to productive citizenship. They need to level the playing field so that every child has an equal opportunity to learn and to succeed. In addition, educators may experience extreme pressure to compete with other educators from within their systems and beyond to the global community in efforts to raise student achievement.

Standards-based education has been part of the answer to questions such as these. Specific content standards now indicate what students must know and do at each grade level. In many cases, educators have aligned these standards with evaluation procedures—local assessments and standardized tests. The stakes, however, are high. Educational funding and teachers' reputations are on the line.

Two points complicate the issue: written standards are not necessarily well developed, and testing does not necessarily align with standards. Many teachers are frustrated and feel like they are teaching in a pressure cooker. The demands for teachers to cover the standards and for students to perform well on standardized measures are overwhelming. It is enough to take the joy out of teaching. Not coincidentally, teachers are leaving the profession in unprecedented droves.

Lost in the conversations about accountability are questions like these that are dearest to teachers' hearts:

- How do students learn best?
- How do different teaching strategies affect learning?
- Under what conditions are students motivated to learn?
- How can we plan learning experiences to optimize learning?

Educators know that when they simply cover required standards, the students are not necessarily motivated to learn. Lessons can be dull and tedious for both teachers and students. There is no time or space to set a lesson in a relevant context. Teachers sometimes dismiss proven instructional strategies that engage students because they feel such strategies are impossible to implement in the climate of high-stakes testing.

Integrated, or interdisciplinary, curriculum—we use the terms interchangeably in this book—has a history of being vibrant and relevant. Yet the advent of standards-based education with its emphasis on disciplines has largely displaced integrated curriculum. Even determined advocates despair that developing integrated curriculum is possible in the current educational environment (Weilbacher, 2001).

This simply is not true. As teachers become more familiar with standards-based curriculum, they are able to begin to integrate areas of the curriculum and are enthusiastic about doing so. These teachers realize that standards are not simply individual tasks that students must perform separately in each discipline. Teachers can chunk the standards together into meaningful clusters both within and across disciplines. Once teachers understand how standards are connected, their perception of interdisciplinary curriculum shifts dramatically. What they once saw as an impossible venture becomes an attractive alternative. Some teachers see it as the *only* way to teach and to cover the standards.

An interdisciplinary approach to standards facilitates the possibility of more creative teaching. The problem is that creative, innovative lessons do not necessarily lead to increased student achievement. Standards can come to the rescue in this predicament. Using standards as the guide, the lessons can be both purposeful and relevant. One of the secrets of the successful integration of relevance and accountability is to work from an interdisciplinary perspective.

The time seems right for revisiting integrated curriculum. Popular in the late 1980s and early '90s as a method to increase motivation, it almost disappeared with the advent of the standards movement. Yet renewed interest is apparent. As Jackie Delong, a supervisory officer from the Grand Erie Board of Education in Ontario, says, "Teachers are now familiar with the new curriculum and ready to make connections."

Many educators are seeing the potential of integration. The Michigan Department of Education and DaimlerChrysler supported a five-year project in nearly 700 schools across 70 school districts to develop integrated curriculum (Warner & Heinz, 2002). Ontario has developed a policy document called the *Ontario Curriculum Grades 11 and 12 Interdisciplinary Studies* (Ontario Ministry of Education, 2002). Students can acquire a high school credit in interdisciplinary studies, a course that focuses on interdisciplinary knowledge and skills such as understanding multiple perspectives, processing information using a variety of research strategies and technologies, and analyzing and describing the impact of interdisciplinary approaches on society and solutions to real-life situations.

In Québec, the Ministry of Education's latest reform effort, collectively known as New Directions of Success, has an interdisciplinary perspective. For grades 1 through 6, New Directions of Success defines broad areas of learning such as health and well-being, personal and career planning, environmental awareness, and consumer rights and responsibilities (*Québec Education Program*, 2001). Identifying these broad areas of learning is "intended to encourage students to make connections between what they learn at school and in their everyday lives, and to provide them with opportunities to develop an understanding of various life contexts and envision possible actions in specific situations" (p. 7).

Other countries are also interested in the interdisciplinary approach. Case studies of integrated science, math, and technology projects in Australia show that such approaches are alive and well (Venville, Wallace, Rennie, & Malone, 1999). Manfred Lang (2003) from Germany currently is working in European countries to implement an integrated approach to science. A key feature of his project is using the collaborative process to decide what is worth knowing. In China, Japan, Korea, and Taiwan, educators developed integrated science curriculum after they realized that the conventional drill-dominated approach to education did not support understanding, creativity, or social interest (Wang & Su, 2002).

In Taiwan, the new curriculum for grades 1 through 9 replaces the traditional subjects with seven major domains of learning. The domains are language and literature, health and physical education, social studies, arts and humanities, mathematics, nature and technology, and integrated activities. Educators designed this curriculum to avoid confining students to the boundaries of a subject and overlooking their ability to integrate learning. The Ministry of Education stresses that the curriculum is humanitarian and promotes moral character. Students learn basic skills through both reading the textbook and integrating the skills into real life. Educators may develop site-based curricula, but they are still accountable for student learning. A goal of this standards-based curriculum is for students to understand change and real life so that they become responsible and contributing members of society. (See http://www.eje.ntnu.edu.tw/l-english /ejeEnglish.htm for more information about the reforms in Taiwan.)

Japanese students do well in international testing and indeed provide exemplary models for their North American counterparts. Yet something is dreadfully wrong: students hate going to school

(Tolbert, 2001). Problems include bullying, violence, and students refusing to go to school at all. They dislike math and science more intensely as they move through the grades, and they lack the ability to do research or to express an opinion. To address this, the Japanese are turning to integrated curriculum.

The Japanese are streamlining the elementary and high school curricula (Tolbert, 2001). Teachers are to devote the extra instructional time to a general studies course with no textbooks and no standardized instruction. In essence, the general studies course is a mandated two hours of integrated curriculum per week. The goal is to teach students how to study, how to conduct research, and how to become more creative.

In Canada's Learning Through the Arts™ (LTTA) program, artists from the community collaborate with teachers to develop integrated curriculum using standards. The program held its first international teacher course in Singapore in November 2002. Hosted by the Ministry of Education, the course introduced 80 teachers to the LTTA pedagogical framework through workshops on holistic curriculum and learning styles. The Canadians also collaborate with teachers in Sweden. (See http://www.ltta.ca for more information.)

We personally have noticed the attention to integrated curriculum from Asian countries. Rebecca's book *Dissolving the Boundaries* (1995) was published in

Korean. Susan's book *Creating Integrated Curriculum: Proven Ways to Increase Student Learning* (1998) was published in Chinese. *Holistic Learning: A Teacher's Guide to Integrated Studies,* coauthored by Susan, is being translated into Thai by the Ministry of Education to be distributed to high schools across Thailand (Miller, Cassie, & Drake, 1990).

This book has three purposes:

1. to provide educators with approaches to standards-based, integrated curriculum that are both rigorous and relevant;
2. to offer proven strategies for implementation; and
3. to validate interdisciplinary curriculum by offering examples of interdisciplinary work that provide data-based evidence of success.

To this end, we offer a generic "formula" for creating an interdisciplinary curriculum and an example of how to implement it in practice. We also describe the work of educators who teach with an integrated approach and successfully address accountability issues such as maximizing student achievement and preparing for standardized testing. Their stories are both illuminating and instructive.

1 What Is Integrated Curriculum?

Innovative educators concerned with improving student achievement are seeking ways to create rigorous, relevant, and engaging curriculum. They are asking questions such as these:

- Can making wind and rain machines improve the reading comprehension and writing scores of elementary students on the Florida Comprehensive Assessment Test?
- Do students really learn math by learning to clog dance?
- When students spend after-school time participating in a microsociety that reflects the roles of real life, will their test scores in math and reading improve?

In Florida, Okhee Lee, an education professor at the University of Miami, engages elementary students in making little wind and rain machines. Students focus on the "big ideas" such as evaporation, condensation, and thermal energy. The Florida Comprehensive Assessment Test (FCAT) does not test science; however, Lee's students have shown more than 100 percent gains in comprehension and writing on the FCAT. Their success in language is particularly impressive because many of the students come from different ethnic backgrounds, and many of them speak English as their second language. Lee claims that when she teaches science concepts she also teaches students to think and write in the structured, coherent ways required on standardized tests (Barry, 2001).

In public schools in Asheville and Buncombe, North Carolina, students learn math skills through clog dancing and explore the solar system through modern dance. In these schools, teachers deliver the core curriculum through the arts. This approach is based on the research report *Champions of Change: The Impact of the Arts on Learning* (Fiske, 1999). This report offers clear evidence that sustained involvement in particular art forms—music and theater—is highly correlated with success in mathematics and reading. Furthermore, at-risk students do particularly well both academically and personally in these types of programs (Blake, 2001).

Students participate in a microsociety in an after-school program at Amistad Academy in New Haven, Connecticut. This program prepares middle school students from a poor minority population for colleges, careers, and citizenship. They attend traditional classes during the regular school day, and after school for a few hours a week, they belong to a microscociety—holding jobs, paying taxes, running businesses, making laws, and punishing lawbreakers. The purpose of the program is to make school more relevant and fun while building transferable life skills. The school raised its average test scores two and a half levels in math and one and a half levels in reading. In 1998, a study of 15 microsociety schools in six states found that at two-thirds of the schools, students posted gains on standardized reading and math tests that were as much as 21 percent greater than those of their peers (Wilgoren, 2001).

In these three examples, student achievement is a primary focus. Teachers maintain accountability while designing learning experiences that are relevant to student interests. Interestingly, two of the schools serve populations of diverse students. In each case, teachers have developed intriguing curriculum that pushes beyond the boundaries of traditional disciplines to produce positive results. Comprehension, for example, is comprehension, whether taught in a language class or a science class. When students are engaged in learning, whether they are taking part in the arts or role playing in a microsociety, they do well in seemingly unconnected academic arenas. These are only a few of the countless examples of students involved in interdisciplinary studies at all grade levels. The examples highlight the potential of integrated curriculum to act as a bridge to increased student achievement and engaging, relevant curriculum.

Defining Integrated Curriculum

What exactly is integrated curriculum? In its simplest conception, it is about making connections. What kind of connections? Across disciplines? To real life? Are the connections skill-based or knowledge-based?

Defining integrated curriculum has been a topic of discussion since the turn of the 20th century. Over the last hundred years, theorists offered three basic categories for interdisciplinary work; they defined the categories similarly, although the categories often had different names. Integration seemed to be a matter of degree and method. For example, the National Council of Teachers of English (NCTE) offered the following definitions in 1935:

> Correlation may be as slight as casual attention to related materials in other subject areas . . . a bit more intense when teachers plan it to make the materials of one subject interpret the problems or topics of another.
>
> Fusion designates the combination of two subjects, usually under the same instructor or instructors.
>
> Integration: the unification of all subjects and experiences.

We joined this conversation in the early '90s. At the time, we were unaware of the long history of educators with similar concerns. In our separate locations, we defined three approaches to integration—multidisciplinary, interdisciplinary, and transdisciplinary. Our definitions of these categories emerged from our personal experiences in the field. We noticed that people seemed to approach integrating curriculum from three fundamentally different starting points. In looking back, we see that our definitions closely aligned with

the definitions proposed by other educators over the decades. The three categories offer a starting point for understanding different approaches to integration.

Multidisciplinary Integration

Multidisciplinary approaches focus primarily on the disciplines. Teachers who use this approach organize standards from the disciplines around a theme. Figure 1.1 shows the relationship of different subjects to each other and to a common theme. There are many different ways to create multidisciplinary curriculum, and they tend to differ in the level of intensity of the integration effort. The following descriptions outline different approaches to the multidisciplinary perspective.

Intradisciplinary Approach. When teachers integrate the subdisciplines within a subject area, they are using an intradisciplinary approach. Integrating reading, writing, and oral communication in language arts is a common example. Teachers often integrate history, geography, economics, and government in an intradisciplinary social studies program. Integrated science integrates the perspectives of subdisciplines such as biology, chemistry, physics, and earth/space science. This type of intradisciplinary program is offered for middle school by the University of Alabama's Center for Communication and Educational Technology. Through this integration, teachers expect students to understand the connections

1.1 The Multidisciplinary Approach

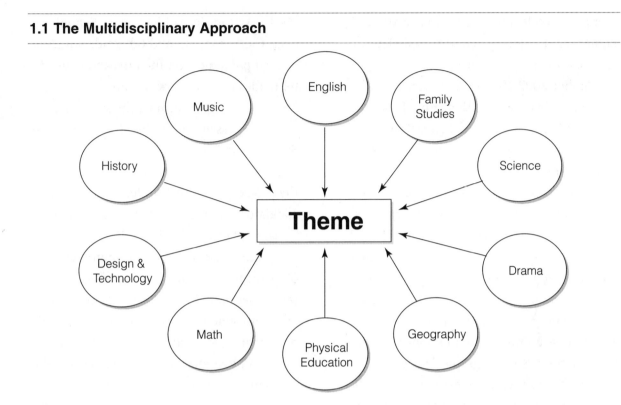

between the different subdisciplines and their relationship to the real world. The program reports a positive impact on achievement for students who participate. (See http://www.ccet.ua.edu for more information.)

Fusion. In this multidisciplinary approach, teachers fuse skills, knowledge, or even attitudes into the regular school curriculum. In some schools, for example, students learn respect for the environment in every subject area. At Mount Rainier Elementary in Washington State, teachers incorporate the theme of peace into every thread of the school's curriculum (Thomas-Lester, 2001). Students begin each week

promising to be peaceful, respectful, and responsible. They follow a list of responsibilities and learn about peace in their classes. In reading, for example, students analyze positive characteristics of people in stories; in social studies, they learn the importance of cultures working together. The school records the number of days without a fight as "peace days"; teachers write the accumulated number of peace days on the blackboard in every classroom. Teachers wear peace signs, and students greet each other with the peace sign.

Fusion can involve basic skills. Many schools emphasize positive work habits in each subject area. Educators can fuse technology across the curriculum with computer skills integrated into every subject area. Literacy across the curriculum is another example of fusion. The November 2002 issue of *Educational Leadership* featured the theme of "Reading and Writing in the Content Areas" and focused on how to fuse literacy into the curriculum.

To prepare students for the compulsory 10th grade literacy test, 9th grade teachers at North Park Secondary School in the Peel District School Board in Ontario developed subject-specific tasks for literacy skills. For example, students practiced skills related to developing supported opinions on disposal of hazardous waste in science, immigration policies in geography, correct approaches to problem solving in math, the influence of peer pressure in family studies, and part-time employment and its impact on teens in business studies. Teaching literacy skills across the curriculum facilitated a low-risk environment for the eventual testing in the next year (Patten, 2001).

Service Learning. Service learning that involves community projects that occur during class time falls under the category of multidisciplinary integration. At Spring Valley School in Columbia, South Carolina, more than 1,200 Spanish-language students engaged in service learning projects. In one project, they distributed 20 tons of food, clothing, medicine, and household products to needy new arrivals in the area with the fastest-growing Hispanic population (Glenn, 2001). At Topa Topa Elementary School at Ojai, California, 5th and 6th grade students created pamphlets on the pros and cons of pesticides to explain how crop pickers can protect themselves against the substances. Students passed out the brochure, written in Spanish and English, to workers and consumers throughout the Ojai Valley. Through the project, students fulfilled state-required standards for language arts, science, and social studies (Ragland, 2002).

Glenn (2001) found that more than 80 percent of the schools that integrate service learning into the classroom report an improvement in grade point averages of participating students. For example, when teachers integrated service learning into the curriculum in a Springfield, Massachusetts, high school, the dropout rate dropped from 12 percent to 1 percent, the number of students going to college increased by 22 percent, and those achieving a grade point average of 3.0 or higher increased from 12 percent to 40 percent. According to Glenn, such programs foster a lifelong commitment to civic participation, sharpen "people skills," and prepare students for the work force.

Learning Centers/Parallel Disciplines. A popular way to integrate the curriculum is to address a topic or theme through the lenses of several different subject areas. In an elementary classroom, students often experience this approach at learning centers. For example, for a theme such as

"patterns," each learning center has an activity that allows the students to explore patterns from the perspective of one discipline—math, language, science, or social studies. As students move through the learning centers to complete the activities, they learn about the concept of patterns through the lenses of various disciplines.

In the higher grades, students usually study a topic or theme in different classrooms. This may take the form of parallel disciplines; teachers sequence their content to match the content in other classrooms. Students often experience American literature and American history as parallel disciplines. They study a particular period of history and read literature from that period. For example, students read *The Red Badge of Courage* in English while studying the Civil War in history. Students usually must make the connections themselves.

Theme-Based Units. Some educators go beyond sequencing content and plan collaboratively for a multidisciplinary unit. Educators define this more intensive way of working with a theme as "theme-based." Often three or more subject areas are involved in the study, and the unit ends with an integrated culminating activity. Units of several weeks' duration may emerge from this process, and the whole school may be involved.

A theme-based unit involving the whole school may be independent of the regular school schedule. At Fitch Street School in the District School Board of Niagara in Ontario, Ellie Phillips and four of her colleagues collaborated on a two-week, cross-grade curriculum unit on the Olympic Games. Curriculum planning required eight half-hour sessions. Teachers grouped students into five multiage classes representing grades 4, 5, 6, and 7. The multiage groups met for one hour daily for nine days. In these groups, students devised a performance task that they presented on the final day of the unit. The teachers observed numerous benefits, such as the following:

- Students exhibited excellent on-task behavior.
- Students worked collaboratively.
- Multiage teams formed within the multiage classes.
- Students were engrossed both as presenters and as the audience for the half-day performance task presentations.
- Students used a wide range of presentation products, such as video, debate, sculpture, and so on.
- Students demonstrated depth of understanding of topics as a result of their sustained interest around various questions (e.g., Are the Olympics relevant today? Does the Olympic creed stand the test of time?).
- Fewer recess problems occurred during this two-week period.
- Teachers enjoyed the process and the results.

Other thematic programs may involve teachers across the same grade. Charles Jervis, Jerry Sauter, and Steve Bull of Auburn High School in Riner, Virginia, have collaborated for many years to teach thematic units in grade 11. They have done this without the luxury of common planning time. One topic they have developed is Exploring a Local Ecosystem from Multiple Perspectives. Students explore the Pandapas Pond from the different disciplinary lenses of science (earth sciences, biology, chemistry, and physics), English (genre readings, analyses, and communication skills), and math (data analysis tools and techniques). The teachers carefully connect the activities to the standards in each discipline. Over time, they have developed a long list of possible culminating activities. They update their Web site continually and use it as a teaching tool with students. The site offers many interesting options for those interested in this type of multidisciplinary approach (see http://www.mcps.org/pandapas/).

Interdisciplinary Integration

In this approach to integration, teachers organize the curriculum around common learnings across disciplines. They chunk together the common learnings embedded in the disciplines to emphasize interdisciplinary skills and concepts. The disciplines are identifiable, but they assume less importance than in the multidisciplinary approach. Figure 1.2 illustrates the interdisciplinary approach.

The children in Florida making wind and rain machines while learning language skills are experiencing interdisciplinary curriculum. They are learning the interdisciplinary skill of communication (thinking and writing in a structured and coherent way). The teacher also focuses on "big ideas" in the concepts of evaporation, condensation, and thermal energy. These concepts transfer to other lessons beyond wind and rain machines; thus, the lesson develops a higher level of thinking than if students simply focused on the wind and rain machines.

Is the example of students learning math and core curriculum through clogging and the arts an interdisciplinary one? Yes, if students are learning skills and concepts beyond the immediate lesson. In Learning Through the Arts™, for example,

1.2 The Interdisciplinary Approach

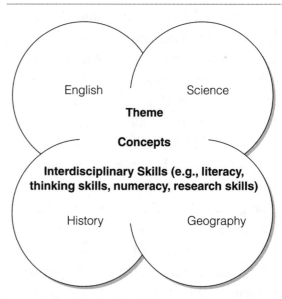

English
Science
Theme
Concepts
Interdisciplinary Skills (e.g., literacy, thinking skills, numeracy, research skills)
History
Geography

students learn math and science concepts and skills while singing, sculpting, painting, and dancing. Artists from the community collaborate with teachers to create integrated lessons that focus on standards. A three-year study of more than 6,000 elementary students participating in this program showed an 11-point increase in math scores among students in 170 schools across Canada. Literacy scores remained the same; however, students reported being happier going to school, and researchers found that students were more engaged in their lessons (Upitis & Smithirin, 2002). The final report and a vivid description of the program are available at http://www.ltta.ca.

At Mott Hall Academy in New York City, students work on interdisciplinary projects that integrate laptop computers. Mott Hall is a math, science, and technology academy for students in grades 4 through 8 who are primarily Hispanic. Every student and teacher has a laptop computer. Teachers integrate computer use into the curriculum, rather than adapting curriculum to the use of computers. In Sandra Skea's 5th grade class, for example, students constructed handmade kites from material such as paper, straws, aluminum foil, skewers, and string. To engage students' imagination, Skea began by reading a story about kites. Students studied such diverse topics as electromagnetism and the use of kite flying in celebrations. They developed a deep understanding of princi-

ples of ratio and proportion as they designed and refined their kites—first on the computer and then by hand. Students also wrote poetry and prose about kites. Skea used the projects as evidence that students not only met, but also exceeded, the standards. She used rubrics to show students how the projects related to grade-level standards and provided the criteria for evaluation. Beyond the academic content, these students learned generic skills related to working together, research, writing, and design and construction (Furger, 2001).

Transdisciplinary Integration

In the transdisciplinary approach to integration, teachers organize curriculum around student questions and concerns (see Figure 1.3). Students develop life skills as they apply interdisciplinary and disciplinary skills in a real-life context. Two routes lead to transdisciplinary integration: project-based learning and negotiating the curriculum.

Project-Based Learning. In project-based learning, students tackle a local problem. Some schools call this problem-based learning or place-based learning. According to Chard (1998), planning project-based curriculum involves three steps:

1. Teachers and students select a topic of study based on student interests, curriculum standards, and local resources.

1.3 Transdisciplinary Approach

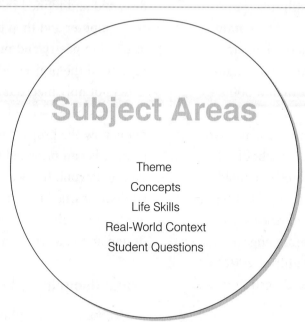

Subject Areas

Theme
Concepts
Life Skills
Real-World Context
Student Questions

2. The teacher finds out what the students already know and helps them generate questions to explore. The teacher also provides resources for students and opportunities to work in the field.

3. Students share their work with others in a culminating activity. Students display the results of their exploration and review and evaluate the project.

Studies of project-based programs show that students go far beyond the minimum effort, make connections among different subject areas to answer open-ended questions, retain what they have learned, apply learning to real-life problems, have fewer

discipline problems, and have lower absenteeism (Curtis, 2002). Newsome Park Elementary School in Virginia, described in Chapter 9, successfully embraces the project method.

At Grand River Collegiate Institute in the Waterloo Region District School Board in Ontario, 11th grade students took on the problem of improving the city image (Drake, 2000). This project did not originate in any subject area; students completed project work in a separate time slot scheduled into the school day. After extensive research, students wrote proposals to renew or enhance the city's image and presented the proposals to a group of external evaluators. Student assessment considered teamwork, critical thinking skills, problem solving, and time management. Interestingly, more than one proposal received serious consideration by the city council.

Negotiating the Curriculum. In this version of the transdisciplinary approach, student questions form the basis for curriculum. Mark Springer of Radnor, Pennsylvania, negotiated an integrated curriculum with students (Brown, 2002). Springer led the nationally known Watershed program for 11 years. His current curricular program is Soundings. In Soundings, 8th grade students develop their own curriculum, teaching methods, and assessments around areas of interest to them. Themes that students have developed include Violence in Our Culture, Medical Issues Affecting Our Lives, and Surviving Alien Environments.

The Soundings program is based on the work of James Beane (1990/1993, 1997), who advocates theme studies revolving around personal growth and social issues. On standardized tests, Soundings students perform about the same as students who have not participated in the program. Parents are overwhelmingly positive about the program, and high school teachers report that Soundings graduates appear to discuss topics at a more sophisticated level than students who have not been in the program. (See Chapter 10 for a discussion of the Alpha program, which is also based on James Beane's work.)

How the Three Approaches Connect with Each Other

When Susan led a provincial team in developing an integrated curriculum, she noticed how her team suddenly shifted into deeper and deeper levels of connection (Drake, 1991). The boundaries of the disciplines seemed to dissolve abruptly. During the early '90s, Ontario mandated integrated curriculum for kindergarten through grade 9. Susan interviewed others who were developing integrated curriculum and reported similar experiences of dissolving the boundaries (Drake, 1993). As soon as they made one set of connections, another set appeared. In Rebecca's context, she found the same dissolving of the boundaries (Burns, 1995).

Describing her experiences to a colleague, Susan discovered there were academic terms for this phenomenon: multidisciplinary, interdisciplinary, and transdisciplinary. The essential difference between the three approaches was the perceived degree of separation that existed between subject areas. Given our experiences at the time, both of us believed that the three approaches fit on an evolutionary continuum. Other theorists have also offered continuums (Fogarty, 1991; Jacobs, 1989).

Standards-based approaches further blur the boundaries of these categories. Multidisciplinary integration might remain somewhat distinct because the procedures of the disciplines are dominant. Current thinking, however, suggests that even intradisciplinary projects should include math and literature/media to be rich and vibrant (Erickson, 1998). Interdisciplinary approaches offer an excellent fit for standards when educators approach them through a backward design process. Although teachers might organize transdisciplinary curriculum around a real-world context, the reality of covering the standards and grading in distinct subject areas quickly brings them back to the disciplines.

Is there an evolutionary continuum? We suspect that obvious differences will continue to exist in the extent to which educators choose to integrate and for how long. We believe that educators will continue to experience deepening connections as they become more experienced in this area. In an era of standards and accountability, no one approach seems preferable. Indeed, they seem more and more alike as teachers integrate standards-based planning with effective teaching and learning practices. The multidisciplinary, interdisciplinary, and transdisciplinary perspectives offer different maps to begin the design process. Teachers can use any of the approaches at any level of education, in a single classroom or in a team approach.

Figure 1.4 shows the relationships among the three different approaches. Some differences in intent are apparent. We found, however, that the educators who actually implement integrated approaches are the same educators who are interested in the most effective ways to teach. They are the ones who constantly ask, "How can I engage all of my students in this learning?" They also are the ones who use the most effective planning strategies, such as a backward design process, and are concerned with authentic assessment practices. Therefore, despite some differences in the degree and the intent of integration, the three approaches share many similarities. The centrality of standards and the need for accountability bring the three approaches closer together in practice.

In this book, we focus on the basics of good curriculum design that apply regardless of the degree of integration an educator may wish to embrace. In other words, the principles we present are worthy of any curriculum design. In addition, all the examples in this book are standards-based. We believe they offer substantive options for educators to develop relevant curriculum in their own contexts.

1.4 Comparing and Contrasting the Three Approaches to Integration

	Multidisciplinary	Interdisciplinary	Transdisciplinary
Organizing Center	Standards of the disciplines organized around a theme	Interdisciplinary skills and concepts embedded in disciplinary standards	• Real-life context • Student questions
Conception of Knowledge	• Knowledge best learned through the structure of the disciplines • A right answer • One truth	• Disciplines connected by common concepts and skills • Knowledge considered to be socially constructed • Many right answers	• All knowledge interconnected and interdependent • Many right answers • Knowledge considered to be indeterminate and ambiguous
Role of Disciplines	• Procedures of discipline considered most important • Distinct skills and concepts of discipline taught	Interdisciplinary skills and concepts stressed	Disciplines identified if desired, but real-life context emphasized
Role of Teacher	• Facilitator • Specialist	• Facilitator • Specialist/generalist	• Coplanner • Colearner • Generalist/specialist
Starting Place	Disciplinary standards and procedures	• Interdisciplinary bridge • KNOW/DO/BE	• Student questions and concerns • Real-world context
Degree of Integration	Moderate	Medium/intense	Paradigm shift
Assessment	Discipline-based	Interdisciplinary skills/concepts stressed	Interdisciplinary skills/concepts stressed
KNOW?	Concepts and essential understandings across disciplines	Concepts and essential understandings across disciplines	Concepts and essential understandings across disciplines
DO?	• Disciplinary skills as the focal point • Interdisciplinary skills also included	• Interdisciplinary skills as the focal point • Disciplinary skills also included	Interdisciplinary skills and disciplinary skills applied in a real-life context
BE?	• Democratic values • Character education • Habits of mind • Life skills (e.g., teamwork, self-responsibility)		
Planning Process	• Backward design • Standards-based • Alignment of instruction, standards, and assessment		
Instruction	• Constructivist approach • Inquiry • Experiential learning • Personal relevance • Student choice • Differentiated instruction		
Assessment	• Balance of traditional and authentic assessments • Culminating activity that integrates disciplines taught		

2 Why Integrate the Curriculum in an Era of Accountability?

Accountability seems to be synonymous with "back to the basics" and the disciplines. The standards in most jurisdictions are discipline-based. For many educators, this means they have no reason to integrate. Yet, most professional education organizations do recommend integration in some form. The National Council of Teachers of Mathematics, for instance, recommends connecting math to real-life situations and to other subjects (2000). Interdisciplinary recommendations, however, seem to flounder in implementation. Perhaps this is because discipline specialists write the discipline-specific curriculum documents. A notable exception to discipline-based documents is the *Ontario Curriculum Grades 11 and 12 Interdisciplinary Studies* document (available at http://www.edu.gov.on.ca).

To complicate matters, educators do not understand curriculum integration well. No clear formula for implementation exists, and no one definition describes the many variations found in practice. Many elementary teachers feel uneasy teaching in unfamiliar subject areas. For secondary teachers, the organizational structure of the departments is a large obstacle to collaborating with others. Yet for many educators, curriculum integration is the path that makes the most sense in the 21st century.

Can We Integrate Curriculum in an Era of Accountability?

In our opinion, curriculum integration is a concept that is well-suited for the times. We believe that integrated curriculum addresses some of the central questions in education today, much as it did in 1895 when the National Herbart Society discussed it in Denver, Colorado. At that time, the Herbartians considered integration as a possible solution to three problems (Wraga, 1996, 1997):

- What is worth knowing, given the huge increase in available knowledge?
- What is important to be able to do, given a huge increase in the number of students needing education to be productive in the workplace?
- How can schools teach moral character if teachers cannot relate curriculum to the real world?

A century later, these increasingly complex issues still characterize conversations about curriculum design. In this 21st century context, we need to add the following concern: How do we ensure accountability in the educational system? How do we know that students have learned what they are supposed to learn?

Interdisciplinary approaches to curriculum begin to address these issues. In Chapter 3, we use the answers to these questions to develop a KNOW/DO/BE

bridge. We believe that this bridge can facilitate the design of integrated curriculum that is both relevant and rigorous.

Ensuring Accountability

What is accountability? This wide-ranging question has many facets. For our purposes, we define accountability as students learning what they are supposed to learn as defined by government mandates. In our school systems, people look to evaluation and assessment procedures to judge this type of accountability. Unfortunately, students' performance on standardized assessments never seems to reach the level that teachers and parents might desire or expect. This leads to the inevitable conclusion that schools and school systems are not doing their job.

In schools that have done well in external evaluation, a key factor for student success is a coherent curriculum. A coherent curriculum means that for teachers and students, the learning goals, activities, and assessments align with each other. Alignment prepares students for both standardized tests and performance demonstrations. According to a summary of research studies completed by the Consortium of Chicago School Research, a schoolwide emphasis on coherence is necessary for success. Schools that had no classrooms or only some classrooms working with a coherent curriculum did not improve test scores. However, those schools that had a coherent schoolwide curriculum showed a 12 percent increase on the Iowa Test of Basic Skills (Gordon, 2002).

As described in this book, the generic process to design integrated curriculum maximizes coherence by beginning with both a vertical and a horizontal review of the curriculum. This review identifies overlaps or common learnings as natural areas for integration; also, it strengthens instructional continuity from grade to grade. Using this process, teachers find it easier to design significant, integrated instructional units because essential understandings from each discipline are included (Martin-Kniep, Fiege, & Soodak, 1995). Additionally, teachers should regularly review student performance data (both for classroom and standardized assessments) to identify particular skills and concepts that need greater emphasis.

Ensuring Relevancy

For many teachers, the strength of interdisciplinary curriculum is that teachers can set it in a context that is relevant to students and fits their needs (Hargreaves, 2001). Two popular strategies for increasing relevance are (1) to begin with student-generated questions and (2) to set the learning in a local context.

Asking students what they want to learn is a teaching strategy found in more than one example in this book. Marie Ciafre, for example, teaches at Newsome

Park Elementary School in Newport News, Virginia. Her 5th grade students choose an integrated topic to explore. She reports higher levels of student engagement and achievement when they are answering their own questions. To defend their choices, students are required to identify the Virginia Standards of Learning (SOLs) addressed in the project. Marie reports that students now know the SOLs better and appreciate learning them in the context of their interests.

Student-generated questions also characterize "place-based education" (Smith, 2002). Place-based curriculum is set in a local context of interest—be it a social, cultural, political, economic, or natural environment. According to Smith, characteristics of place-based education are the following:

- Students are producers of knowledge rather than consumers.
- Teachers are colearners and guides rather than instructors.
- Student questions are the center of curriculum.
- Teachers incorporate as many subjects as possible into the inquiry.
- Students solve real problems.

Many project-based units have similar characteristics. When a team of teachers at Dupont Middle School in Malden, West Virginia, designed a project-based unit, they wanted students to know more about their community and its history. Although they needed to cover the standards, they wanted the lessons to be relevant to students. Malden is the home of Booker T. Washington, old salt mines, and Cabin Creek Quilts—a West Virginia home-based industry based on an old art form. The teachers began by engaging students in developing questions about their interests in these areas. From student-generated questions, teachers began developing the curriculum. Using West Virginia content standards and objectives, they identified interdisciplinary skills such as inquiry, research, and communication as learning goals and began developing a culminating assessment. Then they zoomed in on specific discipline-based concepts and skills to plan related activities in language arts, history, science, and math. The teachers covered the standards, but they set them in a meaningful context for students.

How do students fare in place-based education? Reviewing recent research, Smith (2002) points to schools where comparative quantitative data were available: "Students who experienced place-based education earned higher grade-point averages, demonstrated better behavior, and scored higher on standardized tests in language arts, math, and social studies" (p. 33).

Ensuring Rigor

Integrated curriculum can be just a series of activities, rather than a rigorous program. To ensure rigor, teachers must avoid the trap of superficiality. During the progressive movement of the 1930s, interdisciplinary work was popular, but critics complained that much of what was going on in schools was activity for the sake of activity. Teachers gave little thought to why they selected certain activities other than that students responded well to them. This perception was one of the major obstacles to the success of interdisciplinary approaches at that time. Similarly, integrated curriculum in the late 1980s and early 1990s came under attack for being superficial (Case, 1994).

Superficiality can still be a problem today. However, when teachers consciously use processes such as those described in this book, they can avoid this problem. Less *can* be more. Students can study a topic in depth when they explore it through different disciplinary lenses. Furthermore, they learn interdisciplinary concepts and skills that they can transfer to other areas of life.

We maintain that creating interdisciplinary curriculum with a standards-based approach leads to a curriculum that is highly rigorous, yet readily adaptable to different contexts. Certainly, the emphasis on local concerns in project-based and place-based learning means that curriculum is necessarily different in each location. However, the scope and sequence provided by the standards remain intact. Content aligns with standards, assessment procedures, and instructional strategies.

When teachers have the freedom to place curriculum in relevant settings, they are often very creative in adapting it to diverse student needs. By addressing individual needs, teachers can help all children achieve at higher levels.

Ensuring That No Child Is Left Behind

Today, teachers face increasingly diverse populations of students. Among the questions facing educators are these: "How do we meet the needs of students at a wide range of ability and achievement levels?" and "How do we motivate all students to learn?"

We believe that integrated approaches can effectively serve all learners. Although interdisciplinary work has long been in the domain of gifted learners who do well in these programs (Tomlinson et al., 2002; Clark, 1988), increasingly we notice that the "at-risk" students do especially well. For example, research indicates that studying core curriculum through the arts leads to increased achievement scores for all students, but particularly for at-risk students (Fiske, 1999).

Similarly, teachers from four Virginia secondary schools who used interdisciplinary, teamed instruction reported greater student enthusiasm for learning, increased participation, more completion of assignments, better understanding of concepts and skills, increased connections across disciplines, fewer discipline problems, and improved attendance. Teachers noticed these positive effects particularly with at-risk students (Burns, 1995, 2001).

In part, the quality of teachers who implement integrated curriculum approaches may explain this phenomenon. In our experience, teachers who choose to implement integrated approaches are teachers who also reach out to engage every student. They are very aware of equity issues and approach the achievement of all students as a personal challenge. These teachers are more likely to consider, for example, multiple intelligences, learning styles, and differentiated instruction—approaches that optimize learning for individuals and level the playing field.

Preparing Students for the Next Level of Education

The Eight Year Study in the 1930s provides strong evidence that students can learn through integrated approaches and go on to succeed at higher education (Aikin, 1942). Thirty schools participated in this longitudinal study. Colleges and universities agreed to drop their entrance requirements. Schools were encouraged to be student-centered and to teach the skills and social orientation necessary for a democratic way of life. Researchers matched pairs of students (students from traditional schools and students in the study schools) and compared them on 18 variables that included academic honors, grade average, objective thinking, cocurricular activities, and community involvement. Graduates from the 30 schools performed somewhat better than their traditional counterparts did. The graduates who came from the schools that were most experimental and most interdisciplinary in their curriculum were "strikingly more successful" (p. 113).

Today, Mark Springer notes that high school teachers perceive a difference in students who come from his fully integrated 8th grade Soundings program (Brown, 2002). The students can discuss curriculum topics at a more sophisticated level. Similarly, parents of the Alpha middle school students report that their children do well in high school (see Chapter 10). The students learn differently than their peers; they do not necessarily know all the facts, but they know how to ask the questions. They are goal-directed and can plan how to reach their goals.

How Do Students and Teachers Respond?

Because students and teachers are the individuals who are immersed in the curriculum day to day, their feelings about the curriculum—whether integrated or not—contribute to its successful implementation. Our interactions with students and teachers indicate that integrated curriculum has widespread appeal.

Student Response to Integrated Approaches

Student response to integrated curriculum is usually very positive. Consider the following comments:

> We're what? Learning math? This isn't math; it's art. Math is boring, but I could do this all day. (Grade 2 student)

> I found the unit very enjoyable. I learned a lot about real life that I will never forget. I would like to take part in this unit again. (High school student)

> This is a great way to learn about nature. This is great. (Middle school student)

> I learned more than twice as much as I did before and much more worthwhile stuff. (High school student)

> I learned how to research. (Middle school student)

> I liked this unit because the integration helped me to remember what I learned. (Grade 4 student)

> I learned how to be dependable for others. (Grade 4 student)

Students are, for the most part, enthusiastic about their learning. They talk about three distinct aspects: learning content, learning social skills, and doing interesting activities. The most consistent comment teachers hear is that the unit was "fun." Moreover, teacher observations of how much the students have learned corroborate the students' enthusiasm.

As educators, we need to remember that teacher-constructed connections are not necessarily the connections students make. Using a card-sort strategy, Findley (2002) asked 5th grade students to make connections among the things they had learned during their integrated units that year. She gave students index cards that contained the titles of history eras they had studied. She added cards that represented the literature topics they had explored. Finally, she included a card labeled "Me and my life." Students sorted the cards in any way they wished to make connections. She found that students made connections differently. A previously indifferent student, for example, was excited to see his life connected to the topics under study; another related only to information that came in narrative form; yet another student saw no connections at all.

Similarly, scheduling classes together does not in itself make an integrated program (Horwood, 2002). Students integrate learning through their experiences during the program. Horwood illustrated this point when he explored student learning in Ontario's integrated outdoor environmental programs for high school students. These programs immersed students in a one-semester, all-day program that integrated as many as four credits. Students were pleased with their experiences, yet their significant learning was not exactly what the teachers had planned. Students reported they learned three major things that went beyond the disciplines. They discovered that they could not escape the consequences of their personal planning for a

trip—for better or worse. They also experienced personal growth and a sense of awe and wonder for people, events, and nature.

The bottom line seems to be that integration itself does not lead to a relevant curriculum. In general, students report being motivated when the curriculum is personally meaningful and they construct new meanings about themselves and their world (Erlandson & McVittie, 2001). Students tell us that they learn in supportive environments when they believe the teacher likes them and when they are engaged in experiential tasks (Muir, 2001). Students enjoy and learn from curriculum that is "fun" and offers choice and group work. They appreciate real-world situations and working in depth on projects or inquiries. They like opportunities to learn generic skills and social skills. Above all, Muir's students remind us that good learning is learning that is useful to them. Although we find these characteristics in many classrooms, they are often the hallmarks of an integrated curriculum.

Teacher Response to Integrated Approaches

Why are educators choosing to dissolve the boundaries? After all, disciplines seem firmly entrenched in our ways of thinking about learning. Nevertheless, teachers offer some very good reasons for stepping outside the box. Consider the following voices:

There are so many standards that there is no possible way that I can cover them without integrating the curriculum.

Integrating the curriculum significantly decreases my marking load.

I've read things on brain research and am convinced that students learn best by making connections.

An integrated classroom is a classroom where students are motivated.

The world isn't broken down into disciplines. Integrated curriculum is more like real life where everything is naturally connected. It is more relevant to my students when they can connect what they are learning to real life.

Interdisciplinary curriculum allows me to focus on life skills, as well as the standards we need to cover in each subject area.

Both Melissa Rubocki and Sonja Upton from the District School Board of Niagara, Ontario, claim, "There is no better way to cover all the standards and still make learning relevant." They are far from alone in this perception. Before the standards movement, we heard many good reasons for integrating the curriculum. Now, covering the standards is the first and most important reason.

In an overstuffed curriculum, teachers are looking for ways to make curriculum meaningful. In reality, some teachers systematically and dutifully cover each standard one at a time. Often, this is in response to an administrator who requires teachers to account for when they cover each standard. Other teachers, we have heard, are "bundling and dumping them." That is, they are bundling standards together in chunks that make sense and throwing out the rest. Through integration, teachers can bundle the standards in a thoughtful manner to cover them.

For Julie White of the Grand Erie Board of Education in Ontario, decreasing her workload is an important reason to integrate. For her, marking can be an overwhelming task. When she integrates the curriculum, students work on meaningful tasks in which they demonstrate many different skills at once. She can use one piece of work to assess many different subject areas.

Recently, Julie's class designed dream homes. Students drew the layout, specifying the area and measurement of each wall and room. Julie used the drawings to assess measurement skills in math. Students then drew a picture of their dream homes and received a grade in art. Using design and drawing, they created three-dimensional models of their homes, which Julie used to assess their mastery of geometry concepts and skills. Finally, they wrote a newspaper advertisement to sell their homes. In one activity, she assessed student progress on standards for math, art, and writing.

Janie Senko, also in Grand Erie, believes that a "classroom that uses an integrated approach is a fun place to be." As she describes a recent unit of study, it is clear that her students are engaged in the learning. In reality, the spirit of the delivery is often what engages students in interdisciplinary approaches; integrated curriculum poorly delivered can be as deadly as any other curriculum. Teachers like Janie Senko, who approach curriculum from this perspective, tend to be aware of effective motivational strategies and plan their lessons accordingly. They believe that learning can be fun and rigorous at the same time.

Dianne Stevens of the Ontario Institute for Studies in Education (OISE) of the University of Toronto is convinced that knowledge must have a context if it is to be meaningful. Without meaning, students turn off. Integrating the curriculum in a real-life context makes it easier to see how school knowledge may be useful. In Dianne's experience, students engage more fully with integrated curriculum than with learning confined to traditional subject areas. "When this happens, behavior problems decrease and marks increase. Everyone is happy—students, teacher, parents, and administration."

Many teachers teach not simply to impart facts and skills, but to prepare students for life as productive citizens. Hargreaves and Moore (2000) interviewed teachers who used integrated approaches. The teachers reported positive student outcomes such as higher-order thinking, applying knowledge to solve real problems, collaborating, and being creative.

Kiran Purohit and Christopher Walsh work in a small school in New York City's Chinatown. They collaborated to develop interdisciplinary curriculum in which middle school students consider real-life problems. Students take stands on issues, participate in democratic life, and tackle the problems in a cooperative and interdependent atmosphere. The focus is on students learning to be critical thinkers so that they can better represent their community in real life (Albright, Purohit, & Walsh, 2001).

Recent research on the brain affirms what many teachers know experientially. Students learn by making connections; the more connections they can make, the more they learn (Caine & Caine, 1997; Jensen, 1998). Diana Tomlinson, from the Elementary Teachers Federation of Ontario, believes that brain research and its implications offer a particularly important reason to integrate the curriculum. For Diana, the brain does not have separate compartments for different subject areas. Rather, it is like a roadmap where everything interconnects. For her, integrated curriculum should be the dominant mode of delivery for younger students who are building knowledge networks for the rest of their lives.

Teacher Response to Working Together

A crucial concern today is that teachers are leaving the profession in unprecedented numbers. According to Hargreaves (2001), this is due, in part, to lack of opportunities for creative teaching. Working with others on interdisciplinary projects allows for creativity and professional growth and helps keep teachers in the profession.

When teachers who use interdisciplinary approaches talk about integrating curriculum, they usually speak with passion. Typically, we hear comments such as this one:

> I find planning with other teachers to be so invigorating. My enthusiasm must transfer to the students, because they love it when we do interdisciplinary units. And the parents are pleased to see the students so excited and involved.

One of the greatest rewards of interdisciplinary work comes when teachers do it collaboratively. Collaboration leads to an energized teaching force. Teacher Rob McDowell is typical in his enthusiasm. He postponed his retirement because he experienced a feeling of renewal while working with his colleagues on integrated curriculum.

We have worked with other educators to develop and to implement integrated curriculum for more than a decade. The most consistent reaction we have heard is, "It was the most exhausting but most exciting thing I have ever done." Fortunately, once teachers have experience thinking in interdisciplinary ways, they find that the process becomes easier each time they use it. Many teachers agree with Janie Senko: "I could not teach in any other way."

The History of Interdisciplinary Work

One of the biggest obstacles to implementing interdisciplinary work is the perception that students exposed to it are no more than guinea pigs. However, interdisciplinary approaches have a rich history that spans more than a century.

Curriculum integration began in the late 1800s with the Herbartians, a movement named after German philosopher and educator Johann Friedrich Herbart. Herbart developed the idea of correlating disconnected subject areas around themes, sometimes referred to as "integration of studies" (Klein, 2002). In the 1920s, John Dewey led the Progressive movement; progressive education placed students' personal and social concerns at the center of curriculum. The term "integrated curriculum" also described the project approach in the 1920s, the core curriculum movement in the 1930s, and the problem-centered core curricula of the 1940s and 1950s. In fact, core curriculum and team teaching have been components of middle schools since their inception around the turn of the century.

During the 1980s and 1990s, "curriculum integration" referred to multidisciplinary, interdisciplinary, and transdisciplinary curriculum designs such as those described in Chapter 1 (see, for example, Burns, 1995; Drake, 1993; Fogarty, 1991; Jacobs, 1989). Early childhood educators and proponents of outcome-based education were using integrated approaches because they believed that students could not attain higher levels of learning in a separate-subject approach (Klein, 2002). The National Middle School Association promoted interdisciplinary organization as a key feature of middle schools (Beane, 1990/1993). The project approach, advocated by Theodore Sizer's Coalition of Essential Schools, and the brain-based approach (Caine & Caine, 1991) also stimulated resurgence of integrated curriculum.

More recently, integrated curriculum has been associated with school reform. In one recent study, three-fourths of "restructuring" schools were engaged in interdisciplinary programs (Grossman, Wineburg, & Beers, 2000, p. 1). "Interdisciplinary approaches have become more important today because the needs they serve, although varied and even conflicting, are pervasive" (Klein, 2002, p. 9).

Supporting Research

Some people wonder whether there is enough quantitative research to justify integrated approaches. According to some researchers, such as Wineburg and Grossman (2000), a body of research that attests to better learning in interdisciplinary programs than in traditional ones does not exist. We believe, however, that it is important to reconsider this perception.

Most research on interdisciplinary programs is anecdotal. For the most part, the anecdotal evidence is extremely positive. Yet, this does not impress those who are concerned with accountability and numbers. How do students perform on standardized measures? Some educators raise valid arguments about whether or not standardized tests measure real learning. In the age of accountability, however, students need to demonstrate a high level of academic achievement—whether they acquire it in integrated programs or through other approaches.

Fortunately, there is a growing quantitative database to support interdisciplinary approaches. Gordon Vars spent a career collecting data to support interdisciplinary approaches. His research indicates that students do as well as, or better than, students in traditional classes (Vars, 2000, 2001a). Deborah Hartzler's research goes further. She completed a meta-analysis of 30 studies that included substantive data. Her conclusion was that students in integrated programs consistently outperformed students in traditional classes on national standardized tests, statewide testing programs, and program-developed assessment (Hartzler, 2000).

Other large-scale research supports integrated approaches. The research report *Champions of Change: The Impact of the Arts on Learning* (Fiske, 1999) offers convincing evidence from a database of 25,000 students that arts-integrated curricula lead to high levels of academic success. In particular, sustained levels of participation in music and theater are highly correlated with success in reading and math. The most significant difference is with low-income students. A Canadian study involving more than 6,000 elementary students reports similar results (Upitis & Smithirin, 2002).

The George Lucas Educational Foundation (GLEF) offers a growing body of research to support project-based learning, which is integrated by its nature. GLEF reports that such learning engages students, cuts absenteeism, boosts cooperative learning skills, and improves test scores. For example, three elementary schools in Dubuque, Iowa, showed significant gains in test scores after implementing an Expeditionary Learning Outward Bound program. In this program, students conducted three- to six-month studies on a single topic with a "learn by doing" emphasis. Schools moved from "well below" to "well above" the district average on the Iowa Test of Basic Skills (GLEF Staff, 2001).

We offer these examples because they show a correlation between high achievement scores and integrated approaches to curriculum. Additionally, in this book we provide a number of examples of integrated approaches along with quantitative data on student results that support them. These examples and other recent research come to the same conclusion: students do as well as, or better than, students in traditional programs.

If It's Broken, Why Not Fix It?

In the final analysis, many students seem to be constantly struggling to do well on required standardized measures. Newspaper headlines repeatedly report that students are failing to meet the standards. Yet, in the search for success on external testing, most of the schools across North America continue to use a traditional discipline-based instructional model. Something seems wrong with this picture. If the traditional method is not working, how can we support educators in finding new ways to teach?

Even if students in integrated programs did only as well as their counterparts, the research clearly shows that interdisciplinary classrooms are positive learning environments for both students and teachers (Burns, 1995; Drake, 1998; Vars, 2001a). Furthermore, independent evaluations of various integrated Expeditionary Learning Outward Bound programs indicated

- Significant improvement in student achievement as measured by standardized tests and portfolios of student work,
- Positive change in instructional practices and school culture,
- Improved student attendance and parent participation, and
- Reduced need for disciplinary actions (Expeditionary Learning Outward Bound, 2001).

We selected the Expeditionary Learning example because it is typical of the variety of claims educators make for integrated curriculum. We think the results speak for themselves. Interdisciplinary work is not just about connecting different subject areas. It is about how we do the business of education. Teachers who use integrated curriculum usually create inviting class-rooms that engage students in meaningful learning. They are motivated and passionate teachers. Integrated curriculum can lead to sustained academic success and thoughtful measurement of achievement in ways that actually enhance learning. The time has come to explore how exemplary interdisciplinary practice bridges the need for both accountability and relevance.

3 | Creating the KNOW/DO/BE Bridge

As they design curriculum, educators must determine the answers to three of the big questions of education:

- What is most important for students to KNOW?
- What is most important for students to be able to DO?
- What kind of person do we want students to BE?

The answers to these questions lead to the creation of what we call the KNOW/DO/BE framework. The framework is helpful when working in one discipline, and it is invaluable when planning for interdisciplinary work. An important step for creating the framework—and a rigorous curriculum—is the backward design process.

Backward Design

The backward design process forms the basis for curriculum planning in many countries. We base the curriculum template in this book on the principles inherent in the backward design process explained by Wiggins and McTighe in their book, *Understanding by Design* (1998).

The goal of teaching is for students to "understand" what is most important to know and to be able to do. Understanding, according to Wiggins and McTighe, goes beyond student achievement targets. It focuses on students gaining an in-depth and broad understanding of an area of study, rather than simply memorizing in order to regurgitate material for a test. Wiggins and McTighe stress that such understanding does not simply happen. Teachers need to design curriculum systematically. The authors outline a backward design process that, at its simplest, involves the following three steps:

1. Identify desired results.

2. Determine acceptable evidence.

3. Plan learning experiences that lead students to desired results.

Backward design makes sense. When planners systematically follow the model, the content, assessment, and teaching strategies are coherent. Unfortunately, however, many teachers find backward design to be an uncomfortable process. Traditionally, they start by selecting activities that they already have used successfully. They leave the planning and implementation of assessment to the end, often tacked on as an afterthought. Then, the parts of the curriculum do not align. Students may experience a series of enjoyable activities, but the learning has no greater purpose. When this occurs, students miss the "So what?" of the study.

The process we use for integrating the curriculum follows the steps for backward design outlined by Wiggins and McTighe. We address the same basic questions and adopt some of the basic concepts, such as enduring understandings and essential questions. We add, however, another crucial question that allows us to integrate the curriculum: Can standards be organized in meaningful ways that cut across the curriculum? Figure 3.1 shows the steps in the backward design process and the corresponding questions for curriculum planners. In this chapter we cover the first step. Chapters 4 and 5 discuss the remaining steps.

The KNOW/DO/BE Framework

The first step in backward design is to identify the desired results for student achievement. Another way to approach this question is to ask, "What is the purpose of this unit? How do we want students to be different at the end?" We address these questions by using the KNOW/DO/BE framework. Ultimately, the framework serves as the foundation for a KNOW/DO/BE bridge. The bridge connects the disciplines and acts as an umbrella to transcend them. To create a powerful KNOW/DO/BE bridge, teachers must determine the answers to the questions we listed at the start of this chapter:

- What is most important for students to KNOW?

3.1 Steps and Questions for Backward Design of Interdisciplinary Work

Backward Design Steps	Questions for Curriculum Planners
1. Identify the purpose and desired results.	• What is worthy of and required for understanding? • How will students be different at the end of the unit?
2. Review the standards to determine how to use them in an interdisciplinary framework.	Can standards be organized in meaningful ways that cut across the curriculum?
3. Determine acceptable evidence.	What is evidence of understanding?
4. Plan learning experiences that lead to desired results.	What learning experiences promote understanding and lead to desired results?

• What is most important for students to be able to DO?

• What kind of person do we want students to BE?

Our original conception of the KNOW/DO/BE framework appears in Figure 3.2 (Drake, 1995, 1998, 2000). We selected a triangle structure primarily to denote the relative size of each category. KNOW is the largest category in the framework. KNOW includes facts, topics, concepts, and generalizations or enduring understandings. It is relatively easy to measure the KNOW—particularly the acquisition of facts—through paper-and-pencil instruments and standardized tests.

The DO is much smaller. It includes cross-curricular, broad-based skills such as communication, research, information management, and other higher-order skills such as analysis, synthesis, and evaluation from Bloom's taxonomy (Bloom, 1956). This category also includes such lower-order skills as memorization and recall. Skills are measurable when they are clearly defined and when students have learned the procedures necessary for success.

The BE includes the attitudes, beliefs, and actions that we expect students to demonstrate. Character education, democratic education, teaching the whole child, and habits of mind are ways that educators address the BE. BE is the smallest category and the most controversial. For one, the quality of BEING is very difficult to measure. In addition, BEING essentially exists in the realm of values and is controversial for those who believe it is not up to the school to teach values.

3.2 The Original KNOW/DO/BE Framework

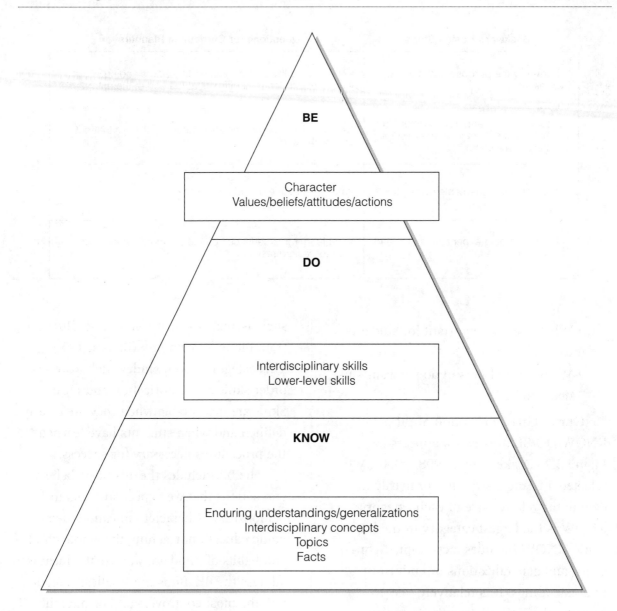

We found that teachers easily identified with the triangle to work with standards. Yet, the relationships among the KNOW, DO, and BE always seemed to generate a large discussion. Teachers seemed to resonate with the BE. They were in the business of teaching young people how to succeed in the world. As Bruce Hemphill, a retired teacher, said, "I wanted my students to learn science, but more important, I wanted them to learn to be good next-door neighbors—to be 'nice' people."

Our schools have focused primarily on academic achievements. The catastrophic events of September 11, 2001, however, led to an urgent call for more character education in schools. Essentially, character education is about being a "nice" community member (see, for example, DeRoche & Williams, 2001). Social and emotional learning programs grounded in a sound research base are emerging to create caring schools (Weissberg, Resnik, Payton, & O'Brien, 2003). Service learning that connects academics to social responsibility is extremely popular (Allen, 2003). The March 2003 issue of *Educational Leadership* was a theme issue on Creating Caring Schools.

Teachers were not comfortable with a representation in which the BE area appeared as the smallest area of the triangle when, to them, it was the most important area. Often, they offered completely different metaphors. Preservice student Jim Penner from Brock University's Faculty of Education, for example, suggested a tree. The foundational roots were the KNOW, the trunk the DO, and the branches and flowering leaves the BE. For him, the fruits of the tree benefited all of society.

Reflecting on the overwhelming response from educators, we changed the graphic. Rather than using just one triangle, we have created one for the KNOW and another for the DO. They act as the supports for the BE. The BE spans the bridge created by the triangle supports. Figure 3.3 shows our shift in thinking.

The KNOW and the DO interact with each other to support the bridge. The triangles must provide a balance for the BE or there is no bridge. What does this mean in practice? To KNOW something, we believe that one needs to DO something active with it. In addition, it is impossible to DO something unless there is some content involved (KNOW). BE reflects what an individual does with the KNOW and the DO. What values do the student's actions reveal? Does he, for example, learn about ecosystems but behave irresponsibly toward the environment? Is she disruptive when she works in a group, although she is learning collaborative problem-solving skills? Are the behaviors that reflect students' values compatible with the knowledge and skills they learned?

3.3 The KNOW/DO/BE Bridge

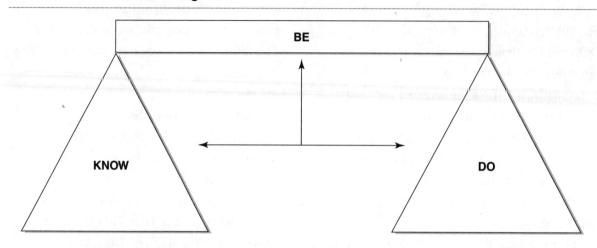

What Is Most Important for Students to KNOW?

Knowledge is now increasing exponentially as a result of the Internet and other technological innovations. It is even more important to sort out what is worth knowing. The definitive canon that prescribed what is worth knowing is lost. There is not enough time to cover, nor is there agreement on, the best possible content. Some subjects such as science are subdividing into smaller subdisciplines in order to incorporate all the new knowledge generated. Educators also are recombining subdisciplines, such as biochemistry.

What is really worth knowing? At first glance, the answer seems to be that we want students to learn the standards. It is not, however, that simple. The standards are often a long list of unrelated items that teachers tend to teach one by one. Students need to know whether some standards are more important than others. In addition, they need to know how the standards relate to each other. We turn to the work of concept-based educators, and Wiggins and McTighe (1998), to address this question.

What is most important for students to learn? Wiggins and McTighe (1998) suggest that not all standards are of equal importance. Educators need to categorize existing standards into curricular priority. They suggest three categories of curricular priority:

1. Enduring understandings (most important)
2. Important to know and do (less important)
3. Worth being familiar with (least important)

When planning curriculum, teachers need to determine what falls into each of these three categories so that they spend the appropriate time on each one. For

Wiggins and McTighe, "enduring understandings" are the highest priority. An enduring understanding gets to the core of the topic studied. What is it that a student should know and remember? What, for example, is important to know years later from a study of medieval times? Enduring understandings have certain characteristics:

- They represent a big idea that transfers beyond the classroom.
- They reside at the heart of the discipline and require active learning.
- They require spending a lot of time to uncover because they are often abstract or misunderstood.
- They engage students.

The concept of a hierarchy of knowledge echoes in the work of concept-based educators. For them, as for us, curriculum is an interaction between content (KNOW) and processes (DO). What is most worth knowing? For concept-based educators, the answer revolves around concepts and the structure of knowledge. What is most worth doing? The answer is broad-based interdisciplinary skills. Some educators weave developmental skills such as literacy and numeracy into lessons at all levels of knowledge. Other interdisciplinary skills are higher-order thinking skills. Higher levels of thinking, however, require working at higher levels in the knowledge structure. To develop critical thinking skills, students must work at a conceptual level.

Like concept-based educators, we believe knowledge and skills are inseparable. We also like to think of knowledge as having a deep structure (see, for example, Erickson, 2001; Taba, 1966). To reflect the structure of knowledge, we envision the KNOW as a triangle (Figure 3.4).

Levels of Knowledge

The Ontario Curriculum provides a basis for the following detailed exploration of the different levels of knowledge. The complete curriculum appears on the Ontario Ministry of Education Web site (http://www.edu.gov.on.ca); it is very similar to mandated curriculum in other jurisdictions.

Facts. At the lowest level are facts. The following examples are standards that require factual answers.

- Identify the way the climate affects how needs are met in different communities around the world. (Grade 2)
- Identify and give examples of three major types of industries. (Grade 8)
- Describe and recognize how different materials affect light. (Grade 4)
- Recognize and describe the primary colors of pigment. (Grade 1)
- Describe and name three-dimensional figures, e.g., cone, cube, sphere, prism. (Grade 2)

3.4 The KNOW Triangle

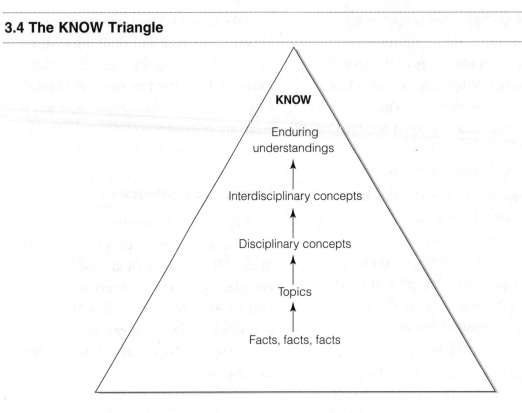

Topics. Topics are the next level. Each topic includes a number of facts. A topic such as the Civil War can involve many facts, such as dates of battles, who fought whom, and who ultimately won. Most instructional units involve a topic of study. The following are some examples of topics:

- Pioneers
- Bears
- Medieval times
- Green plants

Concepts. Concepts act as an umbrella for facts and topics. A concept is a cell for categorizing factual material and can act as an

organizer. Not all concepts are equal. Some are lower-level concepts and may be discipline specific. Others are higher-level concepts and are transferable to other disciplines. The following are some of the lower-level concepts found in the Ontario Curriculum documents:

- Pulleys and gears, photosynthesis, cellular respiration (science)
- Trading partners, imports, exports (social studies)
- Melody, pitch, tempo (music)
- Color, line, form (visual art)
- Character, plot (language arts)
- Measurement, probability, quantification (mathematics)

Erickson (2001) offers the following rules of thumb for deciding if a concept qualifies as a higher-level concept:

- It is at a higher level of abstraction than a fact.
- It has many factual examples within the category.
- It is timeless and crosses cultures.
- It is transferable across disciplines.

Concepts in many subject areas are transferable. "Interdependence" is an example of a transferable concept. It is more abstract than a fact. Interdependence is timeless and is apparent in all cultures. We can find many examples of interdependence in science, social studies, literature, and mathematics. The following are some interdisciplinary concepts:

- Sustainability
- Balance
- Cause/effect
- Patterns
- Change/continuity
- Order
- Cycle
- Conflict/cooperation
- System
- Interconnection/interdependence
- Perception
- Diversity

Enduring Understandings. At an even higher level in the knowledge structure are the big ideas—what Wiggins and McTighe

(1998) call "enduring understandings." For us, enduring understandings are similar in character to concept-based educators' notion of generalizations or essential understandings. They are deeper understandings and can transfer across time and culture. Enduring understandings require a synthesis of the material studied, and they answer the question "So what?"

An enduring understanding or generalization usually involves two or more concepts stated in a relationship. They have the same characteristics as a concept: broad and abstract, universal application, generally timeless and ageless, supported by many examples. They offer a paradox in that they are very simple, yet very deep. We can write generalizations at different levels of sophistication. The following are some examples of generalizations:

- Interactions between humans and nature have political and socioeconomic implications.
- Cultures change over time.
- Cultural diversity can lead to conflict.
- Individual rights balance individual responsibilities to society.
- Different values and beliefs can create conflict between people or countries.
- Failure to resolve conflict may lead to violence.

Many curriculum documents include enduring understandings. Consider some examples we found in state documents:

- Animals, including people, have basic life needs. (Virginia)

- Gathering and analyzing evidence about the world can answer scientific questions. (Michigan)
- Questions often build on existing knowledge. (Michigan)

Enduring understandings are what we want students to remember long after a unit is completed. The purpose of teaching the unit is that students gain understanding of these generalizations or big ideas. Yet Erickson (2001) cautions teachers that they do not need to teach these specifically. Rather, enduring understandings act as a guide to the teacher during lesson planning and teaching.

Principles and Theory. At the next highest level are principles. Principles are different from generalizations in that they are considered to be "truth" and do not need to be tested continually. The law of gravity is a good example of a principle.

At the peak of the knowledge triangle is theory. Generally, the exploration of principles and theory occurs in higher education. Educators in grades kindergarten through 12 are usually concerned with the levels below principles and theory. Thus, the highest level of knowledge that students encounter is enduring understandings.

Interpreting the Knowledge Pyramid

Figures 3.5 and 3.6 offer examples of how educators can use the KNOW pyramid to interpret curriculum documents.

These figures are interpretations from grade 4 science and grade 10 science, respectively, using the Ontario Curriculum documents. The examples revolve around different topics; however, the concepts and enduring understandings are very similar. This illustrates how the higher levels of knowledge cycle through the K–12 curriculum.

Adding a Conceptual Focus

Transferable concepts, not topics, provide a good foundation for organizing curriculum in interdisciplinary work. In practice, however, teachers often choose a topic for a theme. This may be because a topic is mandated or because a popular choice for the organizing center is a piece of literature. A topic does not necessarily qualify as a concept. Figure 3.7 shows the difference between concepts and topics.

How can teachers ensure that they move into higher levels of thinking if they do choose to teach a topic? Erickson (2001) points out that teachers can enrich a topic by adding a conceptual focus. In other words, adding a conceptual theme to a unit topic focuses the topic on a higher-level concept. In teaching a novel, for example, the conceptual theme may be conflict. Figure 3.8 offers some ideas for how to enrich a topic with a conceptual theme.

Susan worked with teachers Sonja Upton, Ellie Phillips, and Melissa Rubocki of the District School Board of Niagara,

3.5 The KNOW Triangle in 4th Grade Science

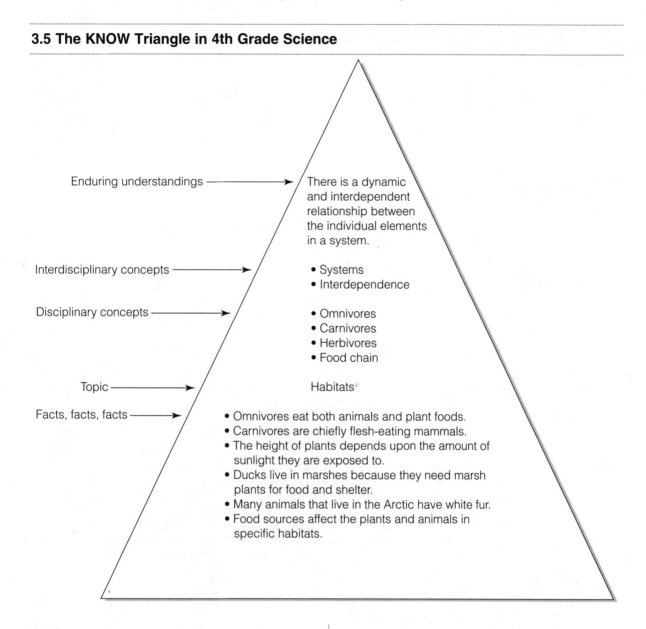

Enduring understandings → There is a dynamic and interdependent relationship between the individual elements in a system.

Interdisciplinary concepts →
- Systems
- Interdependence

Disciplinary concepts →
- Omnivores
- Carnivores
- Herbivores
- Food chain

Topic → Habitats

Facts, facts, facts →
- Omnivores eat both animals and plant foods.
- Carnivores are chiefly flesh-eating mammals.
- The height of plants depends upon the amount of sunlight they are exposed to.
- Ducks live in marshes because they need marsh plants for food and shelter.
- Many animals that live in the Arctic have white fur.
- Food sources affect the plants and animals in specific habitats.

Ontario, to design a fully integrated 4th grade curriculum. One of the units was "Canada"—an enormous topic that could go in many directions. Adding the conceptual theme of interdependence focused the curriculum on the interdependence of the political and geographical regions of Canada. Other possible conceptual themes included diversity within canada or conflict/cooperation among regions. The concept of interdependence appeared in the standards, so it was the preferable choice.

In Figure 3.5, the mandated topic is Habitats. The interdisciplinary concepts are interdependence and systems. To reflect the higher level of thinking, Sonja, Ellie, and

3.6 The KNOW Triangle in 10th Grade Science

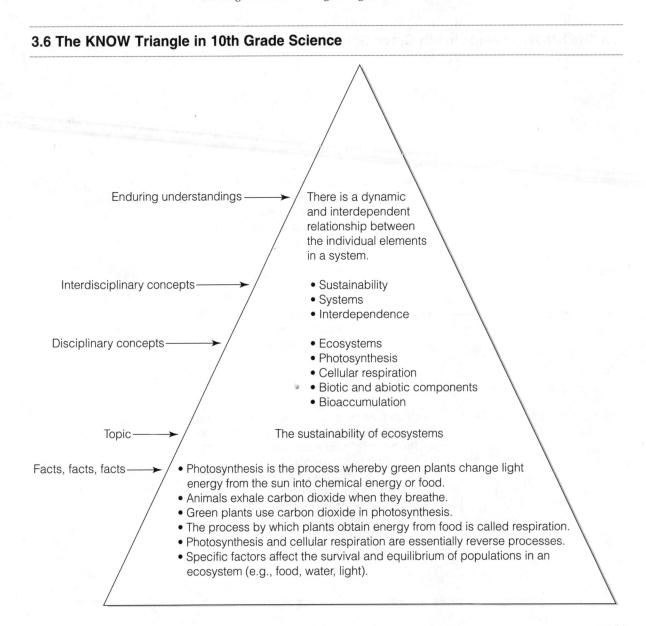

Enduring understandings →

There is a dynamic and interdependent relationship between the individual elements in a system.

Interdisciplinary concepts →

- Sustainability
- Systems
- Interdependence

Disciplinary concepts →

- Ecosystems
- Photosynthesis
- Cellular respiration
- Biotic and abiotic components
- Bioaccumulation

Topic →

The sustainability of ecosystems

Facts, facts, facts →

- Photosynthesis is the process whereby green plants change light energy from the sun into chemical energy or food.
- Animals exhale carbon dioxide when they breathe.
- Green plants use carbon dioxide in photosynthesis.
- The process by which plants obtain energy from food is called respiration.
- Photosynthesis and cellular respiration are essentially reverse processes.
- Specific factors affect the survival and equilibrium of populations in an ecosystem (e.g., food, water, light).

Melissa developed an integrated unit on habitats and added the conceptual lens of balance. The theme of the unit was The Balance of Life. In Figure 3.6, the suggested topic is The Sustainability of Ecosystems. This includes the conceptual lens of sustainability.

Accepting the Challenge

Developing curriculum from a concept-based perspective is a relatively new approach for curriculum designers. At this time, few curriculum documents clearly identify interdisciplinary concepts. In fact, in some documents the word *concept*

3.7 Topic or Concept?

Subject Area	Concepts	Topics
Science	Cause/effect Conservation Interdependence	Butterflies Fossil fuels Weather
Math	Proportion Pattern Ratio	Consumerism Science topics Population, community
Literature	Cause/effect Interconnections Conflict	A novel or story *King Lear* Myths
Social Studies	Conflict Interdependence Belief Culture	Pioneers The Civil War Industrial Revolution The Information Age

describes a skill rather than a concept. Without a concept-based background, many teachers have been working at the lowest levels of the structure of knowledge. Consequently, teachers initially have difficulty determining higher-level concepts and generalizations or enduring understandings.

Moving into higher levels of thinking is challenging. There is a lot of ambiguity and no available list of right answers. The process requires a great deal of interpre-tation. Yet Erickson assures us that teachers can learn to write sophisticated generalizations quickly. She offers detailed steps for creating rigorous concept-based curriculum. For a deep understanding, Erickson's book *Stirring the Head, Heart, and Soul* (2001) is important to read. A less detailed version of this process is available in the videotape program called *Planning Integrated Units: A Concept-Based Approach* (Association for Supervision and Curriculum Development, 1997) and the *Creating Concept-Based*

3.8 Adding a Conceptual Focus to a Topic

Topic	Possible Conceptual Focus/Theme
Dinosaurs	Extinction
Canada	Interdependence
Medieval times	Culture
Consumerism	Cause and effect
Community	Identity
Evolution	Diversity
Civil War	Conflict

Curriculum for Deeper Understanding video kit (Corwin, 2002).

What Is Most Important for Students to Be Able to DO?

What is worth doing? Many jobs in the 21st century require a sophisticated level of occupational preparation. How do we prepare our students? Given such rapid technological change, how do we know that what we teach will be relevant in the workplace? Employers want their employees to demonstrate competency in work-related skills such as reading, writing, basic computation, listening, speaking, creative thinking, decision making, learning how to learn, responsibility for self, and teamwork (Secretary's Commission on Achieving Necessary Skills [SCANS], 1991). These skills are interdisciplinary and are not associated with particular content.

Levels of Skills

It is helpful to think of skills in a hierarchy much like the knowledge triangle. Figure 3.9 shows the DO triangle. In many standards, skills are identified with verbs such as *identify, construct,* and *summarize.* The verb defines the expected level of student performance.

Lower-Order Skills. At the lowest level of the triangle are skills that require students

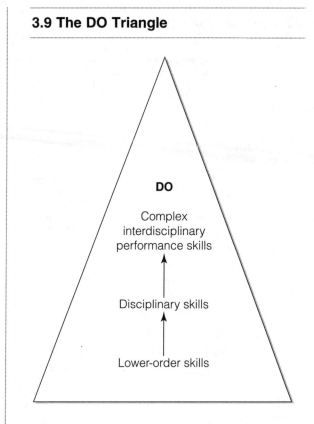

only to regurgitate existing knowledge. Students are consumers of knowledge when they *list, recall, identify,* and *describe.* Many of the standards in curriculum documents are at this level. Consider the verbs in the following standards from the Ontario Curriculum (http://www.edu.gov.on.ca):

- Identify the characteristics of a variety of lines. (Grade 3)
- Describe ways in which artists use a variety of tools. (Grade 4)
- Summarize and explain the main ideas in information materials. (Grade 6)

- Recognize the front, back, and side views of three-dimensional figures. (Grade 7)
- Identify factors that affect solubility and the rate at which substances dissolve. (Grade 7)
- Explain common electrostatic phenomena. (Grade 10)
- Illustrate the cycling of matter through biotic and abiotic components of an ecosystem by tracking nitrogen. (Grade 10)

Discipline-Specific Skills. At the next level are discipline-specific skills. The verbs in the standards are discipline-free, but once connected to the content of a discipline, they become disciplinary skills. These skills may be lower level and not require students to generate new knowledge. On the other hand, these skills may require complex performances and demand that students produce knowledge. Unlike the lower-order skills, discipline-specific skills require students to do something active with the content. Consider these examples:

- Construct and interpret a wide variety of graphs.
- Design and make a pulley system that performs a specific task.
- Compare the characteristics of developed and developing countries.
- Perform the movement skills required to participate in dance.
- Create media work.

- Use the knowledge of poetry to understand and interpret examples of the genre.

Interdisciplinary Skills. Interdisciplinary skills appear in more than one subject area and are often useful in a real-life context; they offer a natural tool to connect the disciplines. Interdisciplinary skills require complex performances; students are producers of knowledge. Here are some examples (expressed as nouns rather than verbs) of complex interdisciplinary performance skills:

- Information management
- Research
- Critical thinking
- Communication
- Problem solving

Figure 3.10 shows examples of different skill levels.

Each of the interdisciplinary skills has a subset of skills. Some are developmental, such as reading, writing, listening, speaking, and computing. Others are process skills that require complex performances entailing a specific subset of skills. Unfortunately, curriculum documents rarely define interdisciplinary skills; nor do they identify the specific subsets of skills. Thus, it is often up to teachers to define these subsets.

One of the most interesting ways to look at complex performance is the SCANS report. In 1991, the U.S. Department of

3.10 Examples of Skills in the DO Triangle

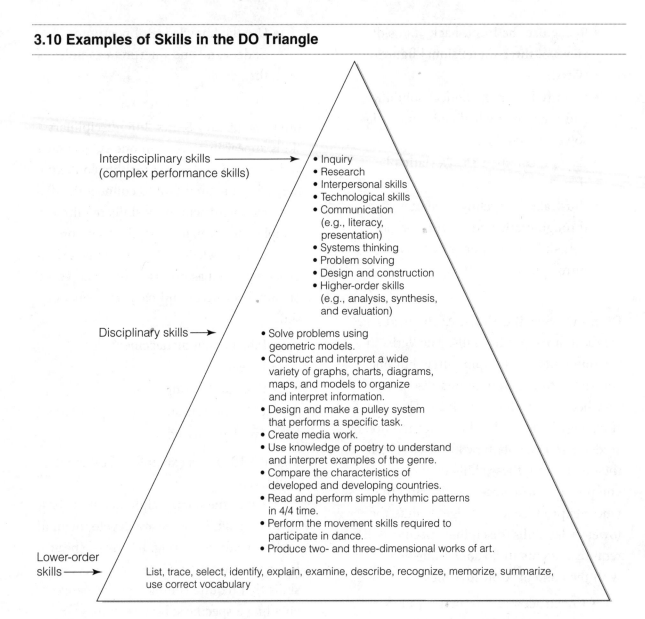

Interdisciplinary skills
(complex performance skills) →
- Inquiry
- Research
- Interpersonal skills
- Technological skills
- Communication
  (e.g., literacy,
  presentation)
- Systems thinking
- Problem solving
- Design and construction
- Higher-order skills
  (e.g., analysis, synthesis,
  and evaluation)

Disciplinary skills →
- Solve problems using
  geometric models.
- Construct and interpret a wide
  variety of graphs, charts, diagrams,
  maps, and models to organize
  and interpret information.
- Design and make a pulley system
  that performs a specific task.
- Create media work.
- Use knowledge of poetry to understand
  and interpret examples of the genre.
- Compare the characteristics of
  developed and developing countries.
- Read and perform simple rhythmic patterns
  in 4/4 time.
- Perform the movement skills required to
  participate in dance.
- Produce two- and three-dimensional works of art.

Lower-order
skills →
List, trace, select, identify, explain, examine, describe, recognize, memorize, summarize,
use correct vocabulary

Labor published *What Work Requires of Schools: A SCANS Report for America 2000* (Secretary's Commission on Achieving Necessary Skills). The SCANS report describes competencies, or complex performances, deemed necessary to prepare someone for the workplace. The report identifies five complex performances and includes the necessary subset of skills within each performance. Figure 3.11 shows the complex performances and the skill sets (with identified criteria) required for each performance.

Who Is Responsible for Teaching Interdisciplinary Skills?

Complex performance skills are often the ones that no one takes direct responsibility for teaching within a disciplinary context. Often educators are not clear about the sub–skill sets necessary for interdisciplinary skills—an obvious hazard if curriculum documents do not make them explicit. In addition, if there is no formal assessment requirement for interdisciplinary skills, teachers usually do not teach them. However, consider the role of skills such as research and communication in effective discipline-based work. Ironically, interdisciplinary skills are essential for successful in-depth work in a discipline.

In addition, teachers often assume that students already know how to do certain skills. For example, teachers often assume that students can present material in an interesting manner; yet students rarely can present effectively without direct instruction on how to do it. Teachers and students need to be able to identify the subset of skills, and students need to receive direct instruction on how to execute them. Equally important, they need opportunities to practice them. The discussion of assessment in Chapter 5 includes an exploration of the criteria for complex performance skills.

Educators do not fully appreciate interdisciplinary skills yet. We believe, however, that this situation is changing and the next iteration of curriculum documents will identify such skills and clearly define them.

Significantly, these skills will be valued when educators also assess and report them. Meanwhile, the classroom teacher needs to take responsibility for teaching them.

What Kind of People Do We Want Students to BE?

How do we want students to be in the world? In the late 1800s, one purpose of schooling was the character formation of students. Would students act in moral ways in the real world? Educators acknowledged that curriculum needed to be more than facts and skills. Today, teaching values is quite controversial. Some curriculum documents even claim to be value-free.

We agree that moral development is primarily the family's responsibility. We do not accept, however, that curriculum is value-free or focuses only on academic development. Building curriculum from standards often leads to a technical and lifeless approach to teaching content and skills. Although we acknowledge that accountability is crucial, we also believe that teachers need time to deal with the big questions, such as what it means to live in a democratic society today, and what it means to be human.

Prescribed standards rarely mention the BE aspect of education. Yet, to dismiss BEING is to abdicate one of our most

3.11 SCANS Competencies

Resources: Identifies, organizes, and allocates resources.
- Time—Selects goal-relevant activities, ranks them, allocates time, and prepares and follows schedules.
- Money—Uses or prepares budgets, makes forecasts, keeps records, and makes adjustments to meet objectives.
- Materials and facilities—Acquires, stores, allocates, and uses materials or space efficiently.
- Human resources—Assesses skills and distributes work accordingly, evaluates performance, and provides feedback.

Information: Acquires and uses information.
- Acquires and evaluates information.
- Organizes and maintains information.
- Interprets and communicates information.
- Uses computers to process information.

Interpersonal: Works with others.
- Participates as member of a team—Contributes to group effort.
- Teaches others new skills.
- Serves clients and customers—Works to satisfy customers' expectations.
- Exercises leadership—Communicates ideas to justify position, persuades and convinces others, and responsibly challenges existing procedures and policies.
- Negotiates—Works toward agreements involving exchange of resources and resolves divergent interests.
- Works with diversity—Works well with men and women from diverse backgrounds.

Systems: Understands complex interrelationships.
- Understands systems—Knows how social, organizational, and technological systems work and operates effectively in them.
- Monitors and corrects performance—Distinguishes trends, predicts impacts on system operations, diagnoses deviations in systems' performance, and corrects malfunctions.
- Improves or designs systems—Suggests modifications to existing systems and develops new or alternative systems to improve performance.

Technology: Works with a variety of technologies.
- Selects technology—Chooses procedures and tools or equipment, including computers and related technologies.
- Applies technology to task—Understands overall intent and proper procedures for setup and operation of equipment.
- Maintains and troubleshoots equipment—Prevents, identifies, or solves problems with equipment, including computers and other technologies.

Source: The Secretary's Commission on Achieving Necessary Skills, 1991, p. 12.

important responsibilities as educators. Values are in the classroom, whether we want them to be or not. Every day, teachers teach personal values by what they say and do, or do not say and do. Any instructional activity that requires higher-order thinking requires value judgments, too. How is it possible to evaluate, for example, without a value framework? In reality, students interact in a value-laden world both in school and out. Yet, this aspect of curriculum usually operates at the implicit level.

For many parents, the BE aspect of the curriculum is very important. A 1998 parent survey at Mulready Elementary School in Hudson, Massachusetts, showed that parents believed that safety and a caring environment, fair treatment, and faculty responsiveness to parental concerns are the top indicators of a successful school system. Academic success ranked fourth (Curtis, 2003). Alpha is a multiage, integrated program for grades 6 through 8 featured in Chapter 10. When a group of Alpha parents talked with Susan Drake, they praised the program with comments such as these:

> The students learn to go beyond expectations because grades are not important (they have portfolios and parent-teacher-student conferences).

> They learn to get along with kids of all ages. They learn to tolerate diversity and work with all kinds of kids.

> They learn to be a part of a community and to take responsibility for their role in it.

Sonja Upton, Melissa Rubocki, and Ellie Phillips from the District School Board of Niagara, Ontario, and Adele Thomas, a teacher educator from Brock University in Ontario were quick to define the characteristics they believed students should exhibit at school. Among other things, students should demonstrate self-direction, reflection, goal setting, cooperation, self-evaluation, being inviting to others, and making good life choices. In these difficult times, these educators considered it particularly important for students to be critical thinkers.

How do teachers bring BEING into the classroom without sacrificing the KNOWING and DOING? For Hilary Brown of the Halton District School Board, BEING is central to why she is a teacher. Brown implemented a human development curriculum for adolescents called Passages (Kessler, 2000). Passages seeks to create a safe container for the wonder, worry, joy, and wisdom within each child to emerge, engaging the student in the learning process. The program recognizes social and emotional learning and spiritual development in the adolescent. Teaching from a holistic perspective, Brown allows choice, creativity, and the use of the imagination to drive her program. She claims this holistic approach nourishes the spirit of the adolescent.

Sonja Upton of the District School Board of Niagara uses Stephen Covey's "Seven Habits of Highly Effective People"™ (Covey, 1990) to develop her classroom rules along with her students. The habits emphasize to her students her concern for each of them as a whole person. Using a commercial planner such as those available at http://www. premieragendas.com, she presents each habit at the beginning of the year in "kid-friendly" language such as "Act responsibly," "Be a goal setter," "Choose to do important things first," "Dare to care," "Excel at listening," and "Get healthy." Sonja then teaches each habit for one week. During this time, students complete T-charts demonstrating what each habit looks and sounds like. They watch video clips and engage in activities that reinforce the habit. Once Sonja introduces all the habits, she structures the activities to provide students with subject matter content and an opportunity to practice the habits of success.

Creating the KNOW/DO/BE Bridge

Addressing the question "What do we want students to know, do, and be?" prepares us to build the KNOW/DO/BE bridge. Figure 3.12 shows the building blocks for this bridge. The KNOW/DO/BE bridge enables us to design integrated curriculum that is both relevant and rigorous.

3.12 The Building Blocks of the KNOW\DO\BE Bridge

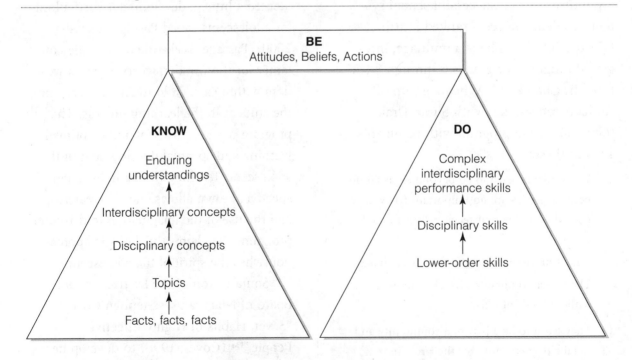

4 | Using Standards to Integrate the Curriculum

Alignment is a fundamental principle of the backward design process and is central to a successful curriculum. However, what does alignment mean? Alignment means that the curriculum is coherent: a common framework aligns curriculum, instruction, and assessment.

Alignment

We believe two types of alignment are necessary: external alignment and internal alignment.

External Alignment

External alignment occurs when the curriculum aligns with mandated standards and testing objectives. First, the written and taught curricula reflect the concepts and skills required in the standards. For example, the concepts of ratio and proportion may appear in the 8th grade math standards in the written curriculum guide. Therefore, the taught curriculum (teachers' curriculum maps and lesson plans) should provide evidence that 8th graders are experiencing lessons on ratio and proportion. At the same time, teachers may note that the concepts of ratio and proportion overlap in science and mathematics. This opens the door to interdisciplinary approaches.

Second, external alignment means that teachers are mindful of testing objectives. Standards and assessment practices can be aligned in different ways. Some states and provinces formally align their standards with standardized tests. For example, Virginia's Standards of Learning tests are criterion-referenced to the Standards of Learning. In some states, however, the state standards do not align with the norm-based test used for statewide assessment. When testing and standards do not align, teachers can refer to specific test objectives and test items to achieve external curriculum alignment. In any case, an informal item analysis of test scores is an important aspect of external alignment. Assuming that the test is accurate, it is problematic if all students from one class give incorrect answers on a certain portion of the test, or on a particular test question. This often happens because the teacher did not introduce those concepts and skills, or the students did not master them. It is important for teachers to decide if the missed questions address significant concepts or skills. In some instances, they may decide that the questions are ambiguous or poorly written. Otherwise, they need to revise the curriculum to include more emphasis on those particular concepts and skills. Teachers also may need to reconsider the strategies they use to teach those concepts and skills.

In our experience, teachers often react negatively to this form of external alignment. They do not want to "teach to the test" but often feel compelled to because of the high-stakes nature of the tests. Given our concept of the KNOW and our commitment to accountability, we are of two minds on this question. We agree that not all standards are of equal value and not all tests of equal worth. Yet we recognize that it is important that students do well on the tests. We can only suggest that teachers be reflective when they make decisions around these matters.

Consider the experience of teachers at Stonewall Jackson Middle School in Charleston, West Virginia. The teachers wanted to improve their students' performance on the Stanford 9 Achievement test. First, they used test-item analysis data to identify the most significant deficiencies. Each day, in an extended learning lab period, the teachers focused instruction on the concepts and skills that the students needed for mastery of the deficiencies. They developed assessments for students to take at three different times before the 2003 administration of the Stanford 9 test. The teachers used Bloom's taxonomy to review their assessments (Bloom, 1956). They found that more than 80 percent of their questions required the lowest level of thinking—recall. However, 90 percent of the standardized test items required students to use higher levels of thinking (Daquilante, 2002). The teachers realized that they needed to align their teaching and assessment strategies with external mandates. This was a thoughtful way to address external accountability.

State- or provincewide testing seems to be a certainty in a context of accountability. Whether or not such testing is a preferred or reliable mode of measurement is unfortunately not up for debate for most teachers. In these situations, external alignment is helpful. Fortunately, we have found that it does not preclude integrating the curriculum. Some of the examples in this book illustrate how this is possible.

Internal Alignment

Internal alignment occurs when the instructional strategies and classroom assessments reflect the language and intent of the standards. To achieve internal alignment, teachers must first know how to "unpack the standards," or decode the performance requirements embedded in them. For example, a science standard may state, "Students will design and conduct experiments." The classroom learning activities and assessments must engage students in the actual designing and conducting of experiments, not just in reading about them in the textbook and answering questions.

To match the requirements of the standard to what students actually "do" in the classroom sounds like common sense. Nevertheless, it is often difficult in practice. It takes an educated eye to read and interpret the standards in a way that leads

to relevant curriculum. Internal alignment is an iterative process. Teachers need to constantly check and recheck to ensure that all the pieces of the standards connect to the actual learning experiences. The section in this chapter on interpreting and analyzing existing standards should be helpful for this task

Clearly, both types of alignment are important for the curriculum in each classroom. Surprisingly, alignment is an even stronger predictor of student achievement on standardized tests than are socioeconomic status, gender, race, and teacher effect (Elmore & Rothman, 1999; Mitchell, 1998; Wishnick, 1989). Alignment levels the playing field for all students and, therefore, is an essential ingredient in curriculum design.

Accountability or Relevance?

An externally and internally aligned curriculum does not necessarily mean students learn as well as they might. Curriculum planners cannot ignore the fact that students learn best when the material is relevant to them. Often the only relevancy a teacher can offer is that the material will be on a test, or that students need to know it in a higher grade. We know that both alignment (and thus accountability) and relevance are possible in an integrated curriculum. Indeed, aligning instruction and assessment with student interests engages students in and promotes retention of learning (Brophy, 2000).

Yet when we worked together on this premise, we found that we were constantly wrestling with tensions that took us back and forth between two seemingly irreconcilable positions. We broadly characterized these positions as accountability versus relevance. At first, we tried to brush these differences aside or to resolve them quickly. The tensions, however, kept reappearing. We recognized that we had to come to terms with them. Figure 4.1 identifies several of the tensions we found between accountability and relevance.

When we considered the tensions to be either/or positions, we found ourselves at loggerheads with each other. When we were able to see them as both/and, our work continued smoothly. Using the metaphors of a zoom lens and a wide-angle lens was helpful. We needed the zoom lens, or a microscope, to see the little picture and deal with issues of accountability. The wide-angle lens helped to explore the big picture necessary for interdisciplinary work. Sometimes we needed to shift back and forth between the two, and at other times, we needed to use both at once.

4.1 Accountability or Relevance?

Accountability	Relevance
We need to cover the standards to be accountable.	We need lessons to be meaningful to students, and the standards aren't necessarily relevant.
We need to follow mandated curriculum.	Students are often really interested in local issues, but these issues aren't in the standards.
We need to think like an assessors when planning activities.	We know some great activities that kids will enjoy.
One-half of the class missed Question 6 on the standardized exam.	We want to focus on big ideas and interdisciplinary skills that students can use for life.
We need to use a zoom lens (microscope) to make sure we are aligning curriculum with discipline standards.	We need to use a wide-angle lens to find the connections and overlaps across the curriculum. Through connections, we can make learning more relevant.

Interpreting and Analyzing Existing Standards

Standards as they appear in curriculum guidelines around the world share some similarities. For one, they are competency-based and concerned with student outcomes. Unfortunately, at this time, the standards vary considerably in quality. Some states, for example, have more rigorous and well-defined standards than others do. This creates an uneven playing field for comparing the degree to which students from different jurisdictions meet required standards. Some states and provinces include standards that are interdisciplinary in nature, as well as discipline-based. In these jurisdictions, it is easier to integrate curriculum.

Educators must deal with standards as they find them articulated in their appropriate curriculum documents. Virtually all curriculum documents are concerned with what a student "should know and be able to do." Most documents do not explicitly name these categories. It is left up to the teacher to unpack the standards to decide exactly what the student is expected to know and to do.

We use the KNOW/DO/BE framework as a way to analyze existing standards. In reality, few documents use the KNOW/DO/BE framework as we conceptualize it. The framework allows a richer understanding of what a standard requires, as written, and opens the opportunity to enhance it in a way that might better fit student needs.

To deconstruct existing standards, it is simplest to remember the following:

KNOW = nouns
DO = verbs
BE = attitudes, beliefs, actions

The chart in Figure 4.2 shows how selected standards from the Ontario Curriculum can be deconstructed using this framework. Analyzing standards using the KNOW/DO/BE framework clarifies exactly what a student has to know to demonstrate the standard. For standards that are written with a lower-level skill, such as "recall" or "identify," only the KNOW is important (see Figure 3.10 for examples of lower-level skills). Standards 1 and 2 in Figure 4.2 fit this category.

When standards move into the realm of higher-level skills, it is important to teach the skills. Standards 3 through 8 in Figure 4.2 require instruction on the skill or the subset of skills required to do the task. Standard 4, for example, requires students to formulate scientific questions about observed ecological relationships, ideas, problems, and issues. Students need to know how to ask scientific questions—one of the subsets of skills for scientific inquiry. It is also interesting to note that these standards are not attached to any specific content—they transcend the disciplines. Most curriculum documents have many standards with similar characteristics.

As previously mentioned, most written standards lack the BE component. This

4.2 Analyzing Standards from the Ontario Curriculum Using the KNOW/DO/BE Framework

Standard	KNOW	DO	BE
1. Identify some of the significant events that occurred during medieval times. (Social Studies—Grade 4)	Some significant events of medieval time	Not included	Not included
2. Describe aspects of the history of modern Western art and of selected forms of African, oceanic, and Central and South American art. (Visual Arts—Grade 12)	Aspects of modern Western art and selected forms of African, oceanic, and Central and South American art	Not included	Not included
3. Collect and organize data on tally charts and stem-and-leaf plots and display data collected by the students (primary data) and more complex data collected by someone else (secondary data). (Math—Grade 7)	Tally charts, stem-and-leaf plots, primary data, and secondary data	Collect, organize, and display data using tally charts and stem-and-leaf plots.	Not included (But objectivity is an implicit value.)
4. Formulate scientific questions about observed ecological relationships, ideas, problems, and issues (e.g., What impact will supplying excess food for a particular organism have on an ecosystem?). (Science—Grade 10)	Criteria for scientific questions, observed ecological relationships, ideas, problems and issues, sustainability	Create scientific questions.	Not included (But environmental responsibility is an implicit value.)
5. Communicate ideas and information for a variety of purposes (to inform, to persuade, to explain) and to specific audiences (e.g., write the instructions for building an electrical circuit for an audience unfamiliar with the technical terminology). (Writing—Grade 6)	Writing conventions (grammar, punctuation, spelling, visual presentation, word use) and writing styles (persuasive, explanatory, informative)	Communicate effectively by applying writing conventions.	Not included (But values are embedded in most communications and certainly in persuasive writing.)
6. Apply decision-making and assertiveness skills to make and maintain healthy decisions related to tobacco use and recognize factors that can influence decisions to smoke or to abstain from smoking. (Health)	Decision-making skills, healthy choices for tobacco use, factors influencing decisions to smoke or not	Develop decision-making matrix and apply decision-making skills.	Though not explicit, values are embedded into "healthy choices"; assumption is to be a nonsmoker.
7. Demonstrate collaborative problem solving, conflict management, and planning skills (e.g., responsibility of each member to carry his or her weight, task analysis, and division of labor, time management). (Social Sciences—Grade 9 or 10)	Procedures for problem solving, conflict management, and planning	Demonstrate problem-solving, conflict management, and planning skills.	Be collaborative.
8. Conduct investigations of the outdoor environment in a responsible way and with respect for the environment. (Science)	Investigation skills	Investigate.	Be responsible, and respect the environment.

does not mean that values are not implicit in the standards. Standards 3 through 6 illustrate how values, though not explicit, are involved in the demonstration of the standard. Consider Standard 5. It addresses effective communication for a variety of purposes to specific audiences. Joanne Reid from the Trillium District Board of Education points out that the standard assumes the existence of such a thing as neutral language. In persuasive writing, however, the writer must assume a value-laden position. Even informative writing is not neutral. Joanne notes that the writer must consider the audience. What is included or left out to appeal to targeted audiences? What words are laden with innuendo and connotation?

In Figure 4.2, Standards 7 and 8 acknowledge the BE. This is rare. We discovered these examples only after a thorough scan of the standards documents. In most standards, as in 5 and 6, the implicit BE needs to be made explicit.

Although accountability mandates require that we cover the standards, teachers have the freedom to expand on or connect to other standards to make them more meaningful. This is particularly true for interdisciplinary work. Making connections across the disciplines through interdisciplinary concepts and skills may not be in the guidelines, but it can enrich a taught curriculum tremendously. Science teacher Roberta Ann McManus uses a number of literacy strategies in her classroom to ensure that her middle school students develop a repertoire of skills needed to read and understand science texts (Topping & McManus, 2002). She teaches science, but she delivers her program through literacy processes. It works for her students. They write journals, read science-related books for pleasure, and practice "think aloud" strategies for reading and writing. McManus believes that people learn through story, and she has enhanced the written standards to practice her belief through an interdisciplinary approach.

Despite the fact that educators feel overwhelmed by the sheer volume of standards, they still need to enhance them when needed. The KNOW/DO/BE framework offers a meaningful way to do this. In fact, enhancing the standards makes them more personalized and thus more doable. In particular, teachers need to be thoughtful about the BE. What values are we promoting in the classroom? Are we designing learning experiences that encourage students to be, for example, self-confident, responsible citizens, tolerant and respectful of others? Teachers may never formally evaluate BEING. However, naming it during curriculum planning ensures that BEING influences the expectations for learning.

Curriculum Mapping

Curriculum mapping is a process for recording the content and skills actually taught in the classroom over the course of a year. Many districts use curriculum mapping as a tool for achieving external and internal alignment. An extremely valuable benefit of curriculum mapping is that it is usually a collaborative venture. In our experience, this leads teachers to rich discussions about curriculum and a deeper understanding of the standards.

Educators use several different ways to map the taught curriculum. Fenwick English (1980), for example, defines curriculum mapping as recording the content taught and the amount of time spent teaching it—what teachers might include in a scope and sequence chart. For Heidi Jacobs (1997), curriculum mapping involves recording content, skills, and assessment in monthly chunks to create a year's curriculum map. Rebecca Burns (2001) believes that the "how" of teaching is equally important and recommends recording the students' learning tasks as well. Using her curriculum mapping process, teachers identify the standards addressed by each task. Rebecca encourages them to use a variety of teaching strategies for diverse learning needs. Using Curriculum Creator, a Web-based tool developed at Appalachia Educational Laboratory, teachers apply her curriculum mapping process to design instructional units. They create learning activities and assessments and link them to specific state standards. Teachers create curriculum maps for each month or grading period that include the completed

units. The sequenced list of units becomes the year's curriculum map and contains all standards addressed throughout the year.

Curriculum mapping includes recording the actual taught curriculum, comparing it with written and tested curricula (district curriculum standards documents and standardized tests), and revising it where needed to ensure coherence. Some states and provinces provide educators with a scope and sequence of concepts (or essential/enduring understandings) and skills with a recommended period for teaching them. Using a curricular scope and sequence makes it much easier for teachers to achieve external curriculum alignment and to create a curriculum map.

Curriculum mapping helps teachers prepare for curriculum integration. Teachers can compare their curriculum maps with the maps of other people teaching the same course or other courses at the same grade. When teachers review scope and sequence documents and curriculum maps across disciplines, natural areas of overlap in concepts and skills emerge.

As the teachers from Lunenburg County, Virginia, illustrate, curriculum mapping is a methodical way to develop a big picture of school and district curricula. It also helps teachers identify natural possibilities for integrating curriculum. Using the state's suggested scope and sequence in each of four content areas, teachers developed their own vertical scope and sequence of instructional units. Individually and in grade-level teams from kindergarten to 12th grade, they mapped what they were teaching into monthly chunks. To identify broad-based concepts and skills, they reviewed the charts horizontally at the end of the year. This process helped them decide which concepts and skills to integrate and what they would continue to teach from a disciplinary perspective.

Figure 4.3 offers an example of a monthly curriculum map. Fifth grade teacher Mary Ann Whitlow from Lunenburg County completed this map primarily for mathematics. It illustrates how Mary Ann integrated language arts and social studies into the lessons by making connections through the interdisciplinary concept of "patterns."

Scanning and Clustering Standards for Integration

The scan-and-cluster process is crucial for effectively integrating a standards-based curriculum. At first glance, it will seem to be a daunting task. Simply reading about it is intimidating. However, it is work well worth doing. *One intensive scan and cluster for each grade is enough.* Then, the scan-and-cluster process becomes second nature. This is not curriculum mapping. Mapping is a disciplined-based activity that works with the curriculum in a literal way to identify what standards are already covered. During the process, teachers identify curriculum gaps and overlaps. Curriculum mapping, therefore, definitely provides a head start for scanning and clustering.

The first step in the scan-and-cluster process is to scan with a wide-angle lens for KNOW and DO—interdisciplinary concepts and skills—that cut across the subject areas selected for integration. A scan is really just that. It is not a detailed journey. It provides the curriculum designer with a big picture. Scanning vertically through the same subject areas shows what students studied in past years and what they will study in the future. The second step is to cluster standards into meaningful chunks. This step needs more detail—the zoom lens helps to zero in on the standards.

To scan and cluster is to review the curriculum using the KNOW/DO/BE bridge as an interpretive filter. Generally the KNOW and the DO exist in curriculum documents, but they are not necessarily obvious. The interdisciplinary skills of the DO are similar in every subject at all grade levels, but they increase in complexity in the upper grades. The interdisciplinary concepts also cut across subjects and reappear at different points throughout the grades.

Some curriculum documents cluster together subskills of an interdisciplinary skill. Alternatively, subskills may appear seemingly at random. The scan-and-cluster process is much like putting together a jigsaw puzzle. The teacher identifies the pieces and puts them together into a meaningful whole. The curriculum documents often

4.3 Example of Monthly Curriculum Map

Grade: 5   Month: September   Content: Mathematics   Teacher: M. Whitlow

Content Standard/ Learning Expectations	Unit/Content	Cross-Disciplinary Connections	Activities/Resources	Assessments
SOL 4.11, 4.12, 4.13 Estimate, measure weight and mass, length, and liquid volume.	Customary and metric length measurement.		1. The teacher demonstrates parts of the body as approximate measurements for real measurements. Teacher demonstrates how to read inches and centimeters. Students pair up to measure heights.	1. Students complete "Measuring Me" profile sheet and decide based on their height and arm span whether they are square or rectangular
5.19 Investigate, describe, extend numerical and geometric patterns, including triangular numbers, perfect squares, patterns formed by powers, and arithmetic sequences.	Fibonacci's sequence. Square numbers. Triangular numbers. Diagonals of polygons. Building apartments (patterns to find 10 apartments).	Language Arts SOL 5.5 Describe the characteristics of free verse, rhymed, and patterned poetry.	2. Teacher reads the book *Math Curse*. Class discusses Mrs. Fibonacci's name and students try to figure out the Fibonacci pattern. 3. Teacher reads *Sea Squares* and helps students build square numbers using orange square pattern blocks, grid paper, and a chart to record findings. 4. Teacher and students build triangular numbers using hexagons (discuss beehives), grids, and recording chart. 5. Teacher reads *A Cloak for the Dreamer* and discusses geometric patterns. Students complete text on p. 271.	2. Students hunt for Fibonacci's sequence in nature—sunflowers, pine cones, pineapples, etc. Bring in examples. 3. Students' grids and charts. 4. Students' grids and charts. 5. Page 271 of math text.
5.20 Investigate, describe concept of variable, use variable to represent a given verbal quantitative expression involving one operation, and write an open sentence using a variable to represent a given mathematical relationship.	Geometric patterns (tiling kitchen homework). Calculator pattern problems. Hands-on algebra lessons.	Social Studies SOL 4.1, 4.2 Time line (patterns in the years on the scale).	6. Teacher and students solve diagonals in polygons pattern. 7. Students find the pattern to solve problem of number of blocks needed to build 10 apartment buildings. 8. Students discuss and solve word problems and calculator problem-solving patterns. 9. Teacher models the set up of additional algebra problems. 10. Students use their hands-on kits to build and solve algebra problems.	6. Diagonal drawings and chart. 7. Patterns quiz. 8. Students investigate the numerical and geometric pattern and then extend it. 9. Transparency. 10. Hands-on class worksheet (kits, calculator, and pictures will be used).

Source: Whitlow, 2001, p. 34.

hold clues for this process. In Ontario, for example, chunks of standards are identified as "inquiry" and "communication."

Most concepts in the documents are disciplinary ones, such as pulleys and gears, or magnetism. Some interdisciplinary concepts also appear in the standards. At other times, it is up to the curriculum designer to enhance the unit by adding a conceptual lens (theme) that can be used as a filter. Some documents identify interdisciplinary concepts in the introduction. Take a close look at the organization of the documents that you are working with to see if they offer shortcuts for this scan-and-cluster process.

Figure 4.4 is a simple depiction of the scan-and-cluster process. The next sections provide a detailed description of the process.

Horizontal Scan and Cluster for Skills

Here are the steps involved in a horizontal scan and cluster for skills:

1. Select standards documents at the appropriate grade level for the subjects you wish to integrate.

2. Identify one interdisciplinary skill—one that involves a complex performance such as research or communication. See the DO triangle (Figure 3.10) for further examples.

3. Identify the subset of skills that are involved in the performance of the complex interdisciplinary skill. For example, research includes skills such as formulating questions, locating information, organizing resources, and so on.

4. Scan the standards document in one subject area to identify specific standards that are a part of the

---

4.4 The Horizontal and Vertical Scan

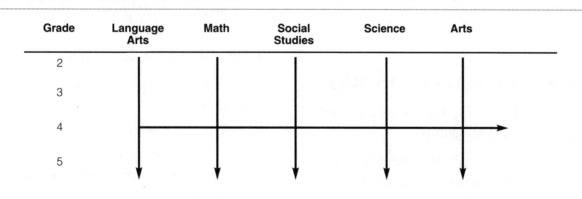

Grade	Language Arts	Math	Social Studies	Science	Arts
2					
3					
4					
5					

interdisciplinary skill. Look at the verbs for help in finding the related standards. In the case of research, for example, these might be verbs such as *formulate, analyze, investigate, plan, and compile.*

5. Choose one color of highlighter. Highlight all standards that relate to the interdisciplinary skill in that subject area.

6. Cluster together standards into meaningful chunks if standards are not organized in this way.

7. Repeat this process with the same highlighter color for other subject areas.

8. Note similarities across subjects. For example, the chunk of standards that describe the scientific method (research skills) in science will be similar in character to standards chunked together under research skills in social studies.

9. Use different colors of highlighters to repeat the process for other interdisciplinary skills across subject areas.

Vertical Scan and Cluster for Skills

Here are the steps involved in a vertical scan and cluster for skills:

1. Select standards documents for one subject area from two grades below and one grade above the one you teach.

2. Scan and cluster vertically through the documents for one interdisciplinary skill (e.g., research) and highlight the standards that address the skill.

3. Note similarities and increased complexity in required performances over the years.

4. Repeat the process for other interdisciplinary skills.

Horizontal Scan for Concepts

Here are the steps involved in a horizontal scan for concepts:

1. Select standards documents in one subject area.

2. Identify concepts that students are expected to know.

3. Differentiate between disciplinary concepts and interdisciplinary concepts (see the KNOW triangle in Figure 3.4 and the examples in Figures 3.5 and 3.6).

4. Repeat for other desired subject areas.

Vertical Scan for Concepts

Here are the steps involved in a vertical scan for concepts:

1. Select standards documents for one subject area from two grades below and one grade above the grade you teach.

2. Scan vertically for disciplinary concepts and interdisciplinary concepts.

3. Consider which of the concepts are transferable to other disciplines. For example, the concept of life systems (science) connects to the concept of systems in government (social studies).

4. Repeat the process for subject areas.

The "Advanced" Quick and Easy Scan and Cluster for Broad-Based Standards

A thorough scan and cluster of the curriculum leads to a deep understanding of the standards and helps teachers chunk them together in meaningful ways. With this understanding, teachers can quickly complete what we call the "advanced" quick and easy scan and cluster for broad-based standards. This is simply a cursory scan to identify the broad-based standards that include interdisciplinary skills and concepts. A broad-based standard may identify an interdisciplinary skill that is wide enough to include the subsets of skills. Alternatively, a broad-based standard may identify a higher-level concept that includes other lower-level concepts. Several standards fall under the umbrella of a broad-based standard.

Consider this standard: "Formulate questions about and identify needs and problems related to structures and mechanisms in their environment and explore possible solutions and answers." This standard is broad enough to include the entire subset of skills for the scientific method when studying pulleys and gears in 4th grade science.

Once teachers have a deep understanding of the different levels of concepts, they can scan the documents quickly to identify the required concepts and to decide how to enhance the curriculum by adding a conceptual theme. The stage is set for integrating the curriculum. The teacher begins the design by selecting one or two broad-based standards for each subject included in the integration.

One Team's Experience

Susan and teachers Sonja Upton, Ellie Phillips, and Melissa Rubocki of the District School Board of Niagara, Ontario, used this process as they prepared to design integrated units for grade 4. The teachers intended to integrate the entire curriculum for a full year. This meant that we needed to use all the grade 4 Ontario Curriculum documents for the horizontal scan and the grades 2, 3, and 5 documents for the vertical scan. The most intensive scan was for grade 4.

To scan properly, we needed to know what we were looking for. We used the KNOW/DO/BE bridge. The scan process gave us a good sense of the big picture. We did not try to examine the standards in detail, but rather used a wide-angle lens.

Because we were all familiar with the standards, this step took us a little more than half an hour. We noted that skills such as research were in every grade and subject area. They just became more complex with each grade. Communication skills appeared not just in language arts, but indeed were in every subject area. Once we had made our general observations, we were ready for the clustering process.

Similarly, we had a lot of discussion around levels of concepts. We found that the categories were not black and white. When one of us defined a concept as lower level, another could defend why it was really an interdisciplinary concept. We discovered during our vertical scan that the higher-level concepts tended to reappear throughout the curriculum. We began to understand why the curriculum documents are not cut-and-dried on these matters (although we believe that curriculum documents need to identify and to provide ground rules on interdisciplinary skills and concepts). Nevertheless, the dialogues were valuable, and we arrived at consensus on what defined a higher-order or interdisciplinary concept.

To cluster, we equipped ourselves with different colors of highlighters for different categories. We looked first for the DO—the interdisciplinary skills within a subject area. We highlighted, for example, all the research standards blue. Design and construction standards were green. Sometimes we had to use more than one color. We

looked first for a skill within a subject area (often found in clusters) and across different subject areas. The interdisciplinary skills we highlighted in most subject documents were these:

- Research
- Scientific method—inquiry
- Problem solving
- Communication
- Design and construction
- Presentation
- Comparison
- Prediction
- Making charts and graphs

Once we got started, this step was quite easy. Figure 4.5 shows some of the standards we clustered together for research skills. We used a set of numbered standards. In most jurisdictions, numbered standards are available. (If the standards are not numbered, it is helpful to number them before the scan-and-cluster process.) In social studies and science, we identified a chunk of standards that presented research skills sequentially (see, for example, 4s29–4s34 and 4z39–4z44). In the other subjects, we found the research skills scattered somewhat randomly in the document.

Now we needed to do a similar scanning process for the KNOW—the interdisciplinary concepts. Unlike the interdisciplinary skills, we knew that concepts might differ from grade to grade. As well, they might not be as easy to spot.

4.5 Clusters of Research Skills Emerging from a Horizontal Scan of 4th Grade Ontario Curriculum

Language

4e41—Begin to develop research skills (e.g., formulate questions, locate information, clarify their understanding of information through discussion).

Math

4m96—Pose and solve problems by applying a patterning strategy.
4m101—Collect and organize data and identify their use.
4m115—Read and interpret data presented on tables, charts, and graphs.

Science

Matter

4s29—Design and make instruments for a specific purpose or function.
4s30—Formulate questions about and identify problems related to the ways in which materials transmit, reflect, or absorb sound or light and explore possible answers or solutions.
4s31—Plan an investigation for some of these answers and solutions, identifying variables that need to be held constant to ensure a fair test and identifying criteria for assessing solutions.
4s32—Use appropriate vocabulary including correct science and technology terminology in describing their investigations, explorations, and observations.
4s33—Compile data gathered through investigation in order to record and present results using tally charts, tables, and labeled graphs produced by hand or with a computer.
4s34—Communicate the procedure and results of investigations for specific purposes and to specific audiences . . .

Social Studies

The Provinces and Territories of Canada

4z39—Use appropriate vocabulary to describe their inquiries and observations.
4z40—Formulate questions to facilitate the gathering and clarifying of information on study topics . . .
4z41—Locate key information about natural resources and their use.
4z42—Sort and classify information to identify issues, solve problems, and make decisions.
4z43—Construct and read a wide variety of graphs, charts, diagrams, maps, and models for specific purposes.
4z44—Communicate information about regions, using media works, oral presentations, written notes and descriptions, drawings tables, charts, maps, and graphs.

Health and Physical Education

4p6—Analyze over a period their food selections, including food purchases, and determine whether or not they are healthy choices.

Arts

Visual Arts

4a43—Plan a work of art, identifying the artistic problem and a proposed solution.

Drama and Dance

4a52—Identify and apply solutions to problems presented through drama and dance and make appropriate decisions in large and small groups.

Few curriculum planners had concept-based education in mind when they created the documents.

The Ontario Curriculum was helpful in some areas. The introduction of the science document, for example, included a chart to identify topics and strands. With our interpretive lens, we wondered how interdisciplinary concepts might enhance the curriculum by acting as a larger umbrella for both topics and strands. Reading the introduction, the intentions of the curriculum designers came quickly into focus. Now we could see the intended continuity for the concepts in the document. Figure 4.6 shows how we used a KNOW/DO filter to interpret two strands and topics for science and technology for grades 2 through 5 in the *Ontario Curriculum Grades 1–8* (http://www.edu.gov.on.ca).

An interpretation of a vertical scan for concepts is similar to a scope-and-sequence chart. Alternatively, it offers a big picture

of the KNOW—interdisciplinary concepts and the lower-level concepts that fit within them. In Figure 4.6, the higher-level concept of life systems acts as an umbrella for the topics of growth and change in animals, growth and change in plants, habitats and communities, and human organ systems. An even higher-level concept is that of systems because it is transferable across disciplines.

Similarly the concept of structures and mechanisms acts as a higher-level concept that includes movement, stability, pulleys and gears, and forces acting on structures and mechanisms. The concept of models is interdisciplinary and acts as an umbrella to them all.

Armed with new understandings, we were ready for the advanced scan-and-cluster exercise—to select one or two broad-based standards for each subject we planned to integrate into a unit.

4.6 Vertical Scan for Concepts

Concepts/Topics	Grade Level	Example	Example
Umbrella interdisciplinary concept	All	Systems	Models
Umbrella higher-level disciplinary concept	All	Life systems	Structures and mechanisms
Topic	2	Growth and change in animals	Movement
Topic	3	Growth and change in plants	Stability
Topic	4	Habitats and community	Pulleys and gears
Topic	5	Human organ systems	Forces acting on structures and mechanisms

5 | Aligning Assessment and Instruction with the KNOW/DO/BE Bridge

In this chapter, we address the last two questions in the backward design process. We turn to assessment to answer the question: How do we know that students learned what they "should" know? Then we explore the final question: What are the most effective teaching, learning, and assessment practices to enable students to demonstrate what they learned?

Assessment for KNOW/DO/BE

How do we know that students learned what is worth knowing? By having them demonstrate what they can DO with what they KNOW. A performance demonstration is very different from asking students to show knowledge acquisition by means of a paper-and-pencil test. Although we recognize that students take these types of tests—and it is important to do well on them—this kind of assessment rarely measures understanding.

How can students demonstrate that they learned the KNOW/DO/BE? A performance-based culminating assessment is the first order of the day. Because an interdisciplinary curriculum focuses on interdisciplinary concepts and skills, the culminating activity should reflect this. This assessment usually is an exhibition, a demonstration, or a project. Students present to an audience that is as authentic as possible. Often parents or other students attend the performance demonstration.

Here are some examples of things that students may do as a culminating assessment:

- Put on a festival for an appropriate period in history and attend in character.
- Take part in a debate.
- Hold a conference.
- Give a workshop presentation on individual or group research.
- Attend a science conference as a scientist to discuss ongoing research.
- Exhibit personal portfolios.
- Present results of project-based learning.
- Display inventions.
- Perform a student-written play.
- Develop an improvement plan for a local organization.
- Design and market a new product.

All the planned unit activities need to align with the culminating assessment to ensure that each student will do well on it. Assessment, however, involves much more than the culminating activity. Assessment incorporated into daily instruction is the foundation of the backward design

approach. Students learn from the assessment itself. It is ongoing, and every activity has assessment of some type built into it. When assessment is an integral part of the learning process, students' learning improves (Guskey, 2003).

Teachers need to think like assessors as they design instructional activities. "How do we know that students have learned what they are supposed to learn?" is a question that echoes throughout the curriculum design process. Assessments should be appropriate, varied, and authentic. Examples of effective assessment strategies include self-assessment, peer assessment, performance, rubrics, journals, portfolios, observations, and checklists.

Connecting Teaching Strategies to Assessment

Incorporating assessment into ongoing teaching activities requires a reflective look at what and how we teach. Teachers need to understand how their choices of instructional strategies determine the skills that students use. The teaching strategy should be appropriate for the skill to be demonstrated. Figure 5.1 shows the link between teaching strategies and the complex performance skills that students need to be able to do. The list also identifies some of the subset of skills that students must have in order to demonstrate the complex performance skills.

5.1 Instructional Strategies and Student Skill Sets

What the Teacher Uses	What the Student Needs to Do
Didactic/Direct Instruction	*Receive, Take In, Respond*
Demonstrate/modeling	Observe, attempt, practice, refine
Lecture	Listen, watch, take notes, question
Questions/convergent	Answer, give responses
Coaching	*Refine Skills, Deepen Understanding*
Feedback/conferencing	Listen, consider, practice, retry, refine
Guided practice	Revise, reflect, refine, recycle through
Facilitative/Constructive/Reflective	*Construct, Examine, Extend Meaning*
Concept attainment	Compare, induce, define, generalize
Cooperative learning	Collaborate, support others, teach
Discussion	Listen, question, consider, explain
Experimental inquiry	Hypothesize, gather data, analyze
Graphic representation	Visualize, connect, map relationships
Guided inquiry	Question, research, conclude, support
Problem-based learning	Pose/define problems, solve, evaluate
Questions (open-ended)	Answer and explain, reflect, rethink
Reciprocal teaching	Clarify, question, predict, teach
Simulation (e.g., mock trial)	Examine, consider, challenge, debate
Socratic seminar	Consider, explain, challenge, justify
Writing process	Brainstorm, organize, draft, revise

Source: Wiggins and McTighe, 1998, p. 160.

Creating Interdisciplinary Assessments

How do you create interdisciplinary assessments? When Susan worked with Sonja Upton, Ellie Phillips, and Melissa Rubocki of the District School Board of Niagara, Ontario, we found the answer linked back to the scan and cluster exercise. During the scan-and-cluster process, we found similar clusters across subject areas. For example, design and construction skills from science connected to ones in visual arts. We noted the similarities between the scientific inquiry chunk and the research cluster in social studies. Communication skills were necessary in every subject.

Armed with this knowledge, we connected the clusters in meaningful ways. When students gave oral presentations of their results from a social studies research project, for example, we could teach and assess communication standards in both language arts and social studies. When they conducted surveys on the demographics of the local area and used appropriate data management for analysis, we could assess students in both social studies and math. When they built castles for their study of medieval times, we could assess them on the design and construction of a three-dimensional work of art, as well as on pulleys and gears for science.

But there was more. How did we identify the DO in the scan-and-cluster process? Consider, for example, research skills. Identifying the research standards is an interpretive task. We realized the standards we highlighted in the documents actually reflected the criteria for a complex performance skill. In some cases, such as in scientific inquiry, we found the skills clustered together in the curriculum. In other cases, we found the standards scattered throughout the document.

How did we recognize the criteria? We did this intuitively, based on our previous knowledge of what a certain skill looked like. We also recognized them, clustered in various ways, in the rubrics we used. Suddenly the pieces fit. Effective rubrics created for interdisciplinary skills identify the subset of skills needed to demonstrate a complex performance. The subsets are the criteria or performance indicators for the interdisciplinary skill. In the rubric, levels of achievement accompany the criteria. *The criteria necessary to demonstrate the DO are in the standards across many subject areas.* This meant that we could teach

interdisciplinary skills and still cover standards in more than one discipline.

To assess interdisciplinary skills, we needed to deconstruct the complex performances into subsets of skills. To create an effective rubric for a complex performance, we needed to use this deconstruction as the foundation for the criteria or performance indicators in our rubric. Examining available rubrics helped identify the criteria.

The Internet is a good source for ready-made rubrics—provided teachers examine them with a critical eye. Sites such as Kathy Schrock's Guide for Educators (http://school.discovery.com/ schrockguide/assess.html) help teachers develop assessment tools. At the Project Based Learning site (http://www.4teachers .org/projectbased/checklist.shtml), teachers can customize rubrics in six different categories: oral projects, products, multimedia, science, research and writing, and work skills. Interestingly, only one of these categories is discipline-based.

Consider the rubric for research that Adrian DeTullio of Hamilton-Wentworth Catholic District School Board in Ontario developed for his grade 4 students (Figure 5.2). He scanned the standards to settle on four subsets of skills: ask a question, collect information, analyze information, and communicate results. Then he developed criteria for each subset in the form of performance indicators. Finally, he added four levels of achievement, as is typically done in Ontario.

5.2 Research Skills Rubric

Level	1	2	3	4
Asks questions				
• *Questions are open-ended* • *Requires research*	Answers require little detail	Answers require few details	Answers require some details	Answers require many details
Collects information				
• *Locates a variety of sources* • *Skims materials*	Locates few useful resources	Locates some useful resources	Locates useful resources	Locates a variety of useful resources
Analyzes information				
Selects pertinent information	Selects little useful information	Selects some useful information	Selects useful resources	Selects a variety of useful resources
Organizes information	Not very organized	Sometimes organized	Organized	Always organized
Summarizes ideas	Summarizes with a few details	Summarizes with some details	Summarizes well with detail	Summarizes well with many relevant details
Communicates results				
Applies required format	Answers the questions with little neatness and accuracy	Answers the questions with some neatness and accuracy	Answers the questions neatly and accurately	Answers the questions neatly and accurately with lots of detail
Uses clear and precise language	Uses little of the proper grammar, vocabulary, spelling	Uses some of the proper grammar, vocabulary, spelling	Uses most of the proper grammar, vocabulary, spelling	Uses all of the proper grammar, vocabulary, spelling
Understands (applies) concepts • Gives complete explanations • Includes opinions • Provides supporting details	Little effort to include complete explanations, opinions, and supporting details	Some effort to include complete explanations, opinions, and supporting details	Good effort to include complete explanations, opinions, and supporting details	Extra effort to include complete explanations, opinions, and supporting details

Source: Adrian DeTullio, Hamilton-Wentworth Catholic District School Board, Ontario.

5.3 A Research Rubric in Student-Friendly Language

My Presentation on the Feudal System in Medieval Times

Due Date: _____

	A	B	C
Research	I gathered my research from books, the Internet, and encyclopedias.	I gathered my information from one source (i.e., books only, the Internet only, or encyclopedias only).	I had trouble finding information. All of my information comes from one book or Web site.
Content	My audience will learn a lot about the feudal system. It all makes sense and it's really clear. I have some great, juicy details!	My audience will get the general idea of how the feudal system worked. I need to add a few more details and examples.	I'm afraid my audience won't really understand how the feudal system worked. I am having trouble making my information clear.
Organization	I know where I'm going. I see just how all the parts fit together. I have used paragraphs and different sentence structures to make it more interesting. My opening will hook you! The ending really works!	My presentation is pretty easy to follow. I have tried to use paragraphs to organize my ideas, but I think I need to move some things around. My beginning is OK. I have an ending, but it doesn't grab me yet.	I don't always know where I'm headed. Sometimes I'm missing indents and paragraphs, and I think I have some sentences that don't make sense. I don't really know what I should tell first or how I should end this.
Presentation	I held my audience's attention by looking at them and speaking clearly and with expression. I felt very good about my presentation.	I looked at a few people in the audience. I think I spoke clearly and made few mistakes.	I didn't really look at the audience. I'm not sure my audience could hear me all the time. Sometimes I spoke very quickly or stumbled over some of the words.

Source: Sonja Upton, District School Board of Niagara, Ontario.

Our group thought the rubric could go beyond the language of the standards. Figure 5.3 offers Sonja Upton's rubric for research, with the criteria written in student-friendly language.

Making the connections among the standards, classroom assessment, and interdisciplinary work clarified a number of issues for us. We better understood how to assess standards across subject areas. When we first began planning activities to cover standards, we started with one subject area and then moved to another. For example, when we designed a unit on Canada, the science activities were separate from the geography activities. This meant that classroom assessment was clear-cut. It was a multidisciplinary approach, and we could check off standards as we covered them. An added benefit was that students could address a problem through the lenses of different roles, such as historian, scientist, or geographer.

Next, we planned integrated activities. For example, students created a Web page to present information on local history and sites of interest. This might involve only standards from science and technology, or it might include language arts and social studies. Creating rubrics based on the standards from multiple subject areas helped students and the teacher see both the distinctions between subjects and the integration of subjects.

Now it was possible to chunk together standards, but also to pull them apart for grading. It was clearer how to report on individual subjects on the traditional report card. These teachers used expectation (standards) sheets to record student progress in individual subject areas. As students covered disciplinary standards through different integrated tasks, the teacher could assess and record achievement in the individual subject areas. Figure 5.4 is a sample chart used to record achievement in one subject area.

Another area of concern was the amount of time needed to create both the integrated curriculum and the assessment tools. This was particularly true for Sonja, Ellie, and Melissa when they were planning a full-year curriculum. Using the scan-and-cluster approach helped address this

5.4 Sample Recording Sheet for Grading Math Standards

Students	Standards										Average Grade
	1	2	3	4	5	6	7	8	9	10	
Jane D.	3	3	3	2	3	3	4	3	3	2	3
Bob M.	2	2	2	4	2	1	3	2	2	2	2

concern. They realized that they could use the research rubric, for example, many times in many units. Similarly, once they generated a rubric for presentation skills, they found it was useful in different contexts. The subset of skills for research or presentation skills remained relatively stable across subjects. The trick was to identify the complex performance skills and their subsets of skills in the standards within and across mandated curriculum documents. In this way, we "killed more than one bird with one stone." We noted that once we created the rubrics, the future time commitment would be much less. *We could use the same rubrics, or slightly modified ones, over and over, and even at different grade levels.*

This experience reinforced the importance of planning activities with assessment in mind. We now had generic rubrics for interdisciplinary skills that needed only slight modifications for different contexts and different content. When we approached a unit, we had to remember that if we wanted higher-order thinking, we needed to work in the realm of interdisciplinary concepts and skills. We also left room for disciplinary skills as needed.

Again, this match seemed easy once we were clear about it. In the unit on Canada, the interdisciplinary concept was interdependence. We built the culminating activity around the concept of interdependence. We needed to ensure that we linked all activities to interdependence and to the culminating assessment. In the planned activities, students needed to articulate the interrelationships among such aspects as culture, economics, and government in whatever area they chose to study. They also needed to demonstrate interdisciplinary skills such as research skills and communication skills. At the same time, they covered standards from social studies, science, language arts, and the arts.

Principles of Teaching and Learning

The final question in backward design revolves around the actual learning experiences included in the unit. What learning experiences promote understanding and lead to desired results? We approach this question from two perspectives. First, how can we structure lessons to ensure alignment with the KNOW/DO/BE and the culminating activities? We used guiding questions to provide this structure. Second, what do we know about how people learn that informs us on best practices for teaching and assessment?

Guiding Questions

An effective practice for ensuring higher-level thinking is to organize learning experiences around a few carefully selected questions to frame the unit (Erickson, 2001; Jacobs, 1997; Wiggins & McTighe,

1998). Then, teachers can organize content around these questions. We use the term "guiding questions" to describe these organizers. Guiding questions act as an overarching bridge across the unit of study. Thus, for interdisciplinary work, the questions must align with the KNOW/DO/BE bridge and with the culminating activity. Three or four guiding questions are enough.

It is helpful to share these questions with students. Many teachers actually develop the questions with their students. Posting the questions in the classroom helps to keep students and teacher focused on answering them during the unit.

Creating guiding questions takes some thought. Like the other processes we advocate in this book, it gets easier with time. A common trap is to ask lower-order questions that only require facts for an answer—a particular hazard if students create the questions. One way to avoid this is to ask questions that begin with "why" and "how" rather then "what," "when," and "where."

For us, guiding questions fall into two categories: essential questions and topic questions. Essential questions are broad, abstract, and similar in nature to enduring understandings. The questions are complex, and they have no easy answers. These questions naturally lead to other questions during the study. Essential questions are interdisciplinary and recur throughout the curriculum.

Using only essential questions to frame a unit does not always work well. The questions may be too abstract to be helpful organizers. In this case, some questions need to focus on the topic of study. These are topic questions. Topic questions are still complex and demand more than one right answer. They lead to interdisciplinary work. Topic questions are more specific and, often, more useful to direct the learning experiences.

Figure 5.5 shows the difference between essential questions and topic questions. We include enduring understandings to illustrate their similarity to the interdisciplinary questions.

Best Teaching, Learning, and Assessment Practices

The last step of the backward design process is to create learning experiences for students that enable them to learn the KNOW/DO/BE. We know teachers are very good at creating enjoyable activities. This is particularly true when a group of teachers collaborate with each other. But we also know that the secret for bridging accountability and relevance is to address the specific requirements of standards through effective teaching and learning practices.

We believe in using constructivist principles for teaching and learning to guide the creation of instructional strategies. In addition, the instructional activities need to align with and lead to the culminating

5.5 Enduring Understandings and Guiding Questions

Enduring Understanding	Guiding Questions	
	Essential Question	Topic Question(s)
Our heritage connects us to the past.	Can we ever be really free from the influence of our ancestors?	How does our society reflect medieval times? How do religious conflicts from the past affect us today?
History has lessons for the present.	Is it true that those who ignore history are doomed to repeat it?	Is it true in recent North American history that history has repeated itself?
Life is considered sacred in some societies.	Who has the right to create/destroy life?	How was Dolly cloned? Should cloning be legal? When is capital punishment acceptable?
A system is made up of interdependent parts.	How can a system survive when one of the parts malfunctions?	How do human activities affect the plants and animals in a local habitat? How do plants and animals affect humans? How do nations promote self-preservation? Should SUV drivers pay an extra tax?
Members of society have roles, rights, and responsibilities.	How do the roles, rights, and responsibilities of different people in society affect each other?	What was the relationship of rights to responsibilities for people in different roles in medieval times? How are individual rights balanced with individual responsibilities in democratic societies such as the United States?
War has characterized human relationships throughout time.	Is war a necessary evil?	What are the root causes of the war on terrorism? What is the moral of *The Red Badge of Courage?*

activity—the demonstration of the KNOW/DO/BE. Finally, teachers need to complement the ongoing instructional activities with ongoing assessment. Teachers should ask, "How do I know when the student knows this?" at the same time as they consider, "How do I make this an interesting and relevant activity?"

A good rule of thumb to use when thinking about best practices is to focus, again, on alignment. If students learn well in a certain mode, then it follows that the teaching strategies and assessment should align with this mode. Figure 5.6 illustrates how teachers can align their teaching and assessment with learning principles.

We could write an entire book on best practices. However, the chart in Figure 5.6 offers a quick snapshot of aligning learning principles with teaching practices and assessment. We aligned the chart horizontally. Each horizontal row in Figure 5.6 deserves a great deal of thought and discussion. Reading the chart vertically is important, too. Effective practice requires teachers to interweave the teaching and assessment strategies mentioned in each row. No one row stands alone. For example, constructivist principles tend to focus on the social interaction of the teacher and student(s) to construct knowledge. This leads to learning in a social context such as group work. This principle does not negate teacher-directed instruction. Direct instruction is very effec-

tive in some situations and with certain students. In addition, using a variety of teaching strategies is very important.

Using the chart, teachers can reflect on whether they are applying principles of learning to their teaching. How do they, for example, do the following:

- Encourage students to participate actively (e.g., by teaching lessons, creating projects, designing experiments, and engaging in self-assessment and goal setting)?
- Address multiple intelligences and cultural diversity?
- Connect the lesson to the real world?
- Direct students to use higher-order thinking skills?
- Provide for student choice and variety in learning activities?
- Align the instructional strategies with the KNOW/DO/BE?
- Provide structured organizers to guide the learning process?
- Present students with criteria (performance indicators) for performance demonstrations?

In a classroom where the best practices of teaching, learning, and assessment exist, the curriculum engages students. In these same classrooms, teachers tend to practice integrated curriculum—whether through conscious design or because using best instructional practices leads to blurring of the disciplinary boundaries.

5.6 Aligning Teaching and Learning Practices with Assessment

If a student learns . . .	Then appropriate teaching strategies . . .	And the aligned assessment strategy . . .
By doing	Are hands-on activities	Is a performance or demonstration
With choice	Offer choice	Offers choice
With relevance	Are personally relevant activities	Is personally meaningful
With structured organizers	Provide structured organizers such as guiding questions—essential questions and unit questions	Provides organizers for assessment—description of performance tasks along with scoring rubrics
With positive reinforcement	Offer positive reinforcement	Offers ongoing, constructive feedback with opportunity to redo
In a supportive environment	Include praise, learning from mistakes, taking risks, constructive feedback	Offers positive as well as negative feedback
Through enjoyable ("fun") activities	Include enjoyable activities	Is enjoyable at times
Through challenge	Expect high standards	Has high standards
With clear expectations	Provide explicit criteria for standards	Has specific performance criteria (rubric)
Through ongoing feedback	Incorporate ongoing feedback into instruction	Uses ongoing assessment with feedback
Through reflection	Allow time for reflection	Uses journals, discussion, quiet time, self-assessment
By teaching others	Value students teaching others (e.g., tutoring, demonstration)	Assesses teaching performance of student
By using metacognitive strategies	Use metacognitive strategies	Assesses metacognition
With variety	Use a variety of teaching strategies including direct instruction	Uses a variety of assessment tools
By the modeling of others	Show the teacher modeling good learning practices	Uses teacher self-assessment and student evaluation of teacher
Through the social construction of knowledge	Use pairs, group work	Uses peer evaluation

Source: Adapted from Drake, 1998.

6

A Template for Planning Interdisciplinary Curriculum

The interdisciplinary curriculum template we provide in this chapter is a generic one suitable for all grades. In an elementary school situation, one teacher often teaches the entire curriculum. This template is very suitable in that context. In high school (or if students rotate to various classes), teachers often choose a multidisciplinary model for integrating the curriculum because it allows them to independently teach their own disciplines. The generic template, however, can also work in this context. Teachers can work together to develop the KNOW/DO/BE bridge and the assessments. Then they may teach ongoing activities independently or as a team.

The sample we refer to throughout this chapter is a modified version of the Medieval Times unit developed for grade 4 by Adrian DeTullio of Hamilton-Wentworth Catholic District School Board in Ontario, Debra Attenborough of the Niagara Falls Art Gallery in Ontario, and Susan. The plan integrates science, social studies, language arts, and the arts using the Ontario Curriculum documents (http://www.edu.gov.on.ca).

Working Through the Template

Figure 6.1 shows the steps involved in designing integrated curriculum. Although the process appears linear in this depiction, it is rarely linear in practice. Instead, it is a process in which the designers need to be able to shift between a zoom and a wide-angle lens—and sometimes to see with both at once. The process is also iterative. To align the curriculum, teachers need to move constantly back and forth between the steps. The first three steps act almost as a warm-up for planning.

Step by Step

Step 1. Scan and cluster curriculum standards both vertically (through grades) and horizontally (across subject areas) to get a sense of concepts and skills being developed over time. Choose subject areas for integration. Select one or two broad-based standards in each of these subject areas. Chapter 4 covers scanning and clustering in detail, and we urge teachers to do this step the first time they plan an integrated curriculum. When they are very familiar with the curriculum standards, teachers can select a few that are broad-based enough to serve as the foundation for an integrated curriculum. Teachers also need to scan the curriculum documents for both subject-specific concepts and transferable concepts. By "broad-based," we mean that the standards are general enough that many other standards could fall under their umbrella. The following are some examples of broad-based standards we selected from the Grade 4 Ontario Curriculum:

- Formulate questions about and identify needs and problems related to structures and mechanisms in their

6.1 Steps for Designing Integrated Curriculum

1. Scan and cluster standards vertically and horizontally to select one or two broad-based standards for each discipline.

2. Choose an age-appropriate and relevant topic or theme.

3. Create a web to identify potential clusters of standards.

4. Construct the KNOW/DO/BE bridge.

5. Design a culminating assessment.

6. Create guiding questions.

7. Generate instructional activities and assessments aligned with the KNOW/DO/BE bridge and the culminating assessment.

    (a) Recluster standards to develop mini-units (if necessary).

    (b) Create standards-based learning experiences with built-in assessment.

environment and explore possible solutions and answers. (Science)

- Produce two- and three-dimensional works of art that communicate ideas for specific purposes and to specific audiences. (The arts)
- Begin to develop research skills. (Social studies, science)
- Identify the distinguishing features of a medieval society. (Social studies)
- Contribute and work constructively in groups. (Language)

Step 2. Choose an age-appropriate and relevant topic or theme. Usually the topic or theme emerges during the scan-and-cluster process and comes from the standards documents. This is fine if the topic or theme is relevant for students. Teachers also should remember that a topic is probably not rich enough to require higher-order thinking, and they may need to add a conceptual theme once they have created the KNOW/DO/BE bridge.

One way to increase relevance is to set the selected topic or theme in a local context. Involving students in the decision making also helps to ensure relevance. Many of the teachers featured in this book have successfully involved students in all or most steps of the curriculum design process. Indeed, the National Middle School Association recommends integrating the curriculum by having students develop their own questions to deal with

particular standards (National Middle School Association, 2002).

Adrian, Debra, and Susan chose the topic of medieval times because it was one of the mandated units from the grade 4 Ontario Curriculum Social Studies document. We also knew it was popular with grade 4 students. It was a *topic*, however, and we would need to consider a conceptual *theme* as we built the KNOW/DO/BE bridge.

Step 3. Create a web to identify potential clusters of standards. It is time to use a zoom lens to determine the content of the interdisciplinary unit. Using the wide-angle lens during the scan and cluster provided a big picture of the curriculum. Creating a web is a good strategy to use when brainstorming for connections. At this point, we find that most people want to cluster standards within subject areas. Figure 6.2 shows a web that can be used to identify clusters of standards in the disciplines. Figure 6.3 shows how we used the web to create the Medieval Times unit.

Step 4. Construct the KNOW/DO/BE bridge. The topic or theme is established. At this stage, teachers have a good sense of how the standards can fit together. It is time to build the KNOW/DO/BE bridge. Figure 6.4 reviews the building blocks needed to construct the bridge. This is a challenging activity, but worth the effort.

6.2 A Web for Clusters of Standards

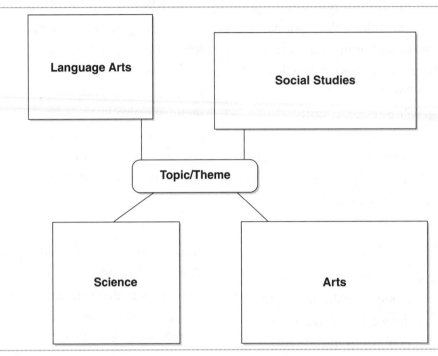

6.3 The Web for Clusters of Standards Applied to the Medieval Times Unit

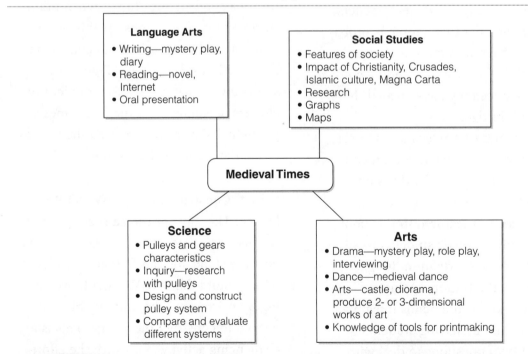

Source: Adrian DeTullio, Hamilton-Wentworth Catholic District School Board, Ontario; Debra Attenborough, Niagara Falls Art Gallery, Ontario; and Susan M. Drake.

Without the bridge, the interdisciplinary unit runs the real danger of being a collection of discrete activities without a purpose. The KNOW/DO/BE bridge ensures a purposeful, coherent curriculum. Figure 6.5 shows the KNOW/DO/BE bridge for the Medieval Times unit.

Step 5. Design a culminating assessment. Once teachers construct the KNOW/DO/BE bridge, the next step is to create a culminating assessment. The assessment is usually a big event, such as a performance, a presentation, or an exhibition that demonstrates what students learned. The culminating activity must connect to the KNOW/DO/BE bridge.

Our culminating assessment was a medieval fair. We invited other students and parents to attend. Students prepared for the fair by making castles, doing research on different aspects of medieval society, performing medieval dances, and writing and acting in a mystery play. They dressed in medieval costumes appropriate for a designated social role. We used peer, self, and teacher assessment to evaluate skills in research, presentation, and design and construction. (See Figure 5.2 for the research rubric that Adrian developed and used to assess the research portion of this activity.)

Step 6. Create guiding questions. Guiding questions focus the learning. They can

6.4 The KNOW/DO/BE Bridge

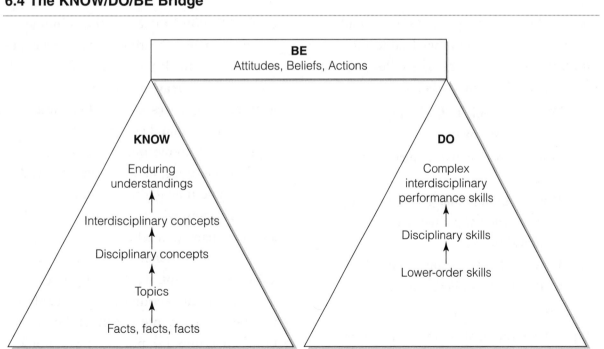

83

6.5 The KNOW/DO/BE Bridge for the Medieval Times Unit

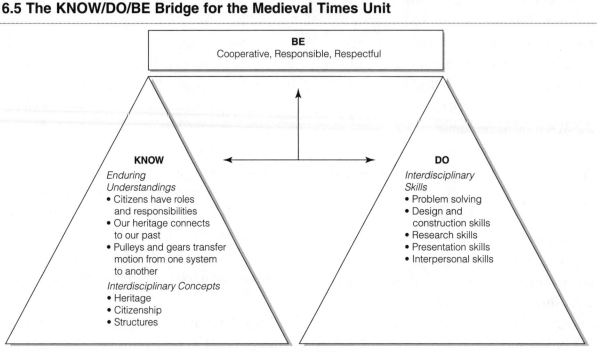

BE
Cooperative, Responsible, Respectful

KNOW
Enduring Understandings
• Citizens have roles and responsibilities
• Our heritage connects to our past
• Pulleys and gears transfer motion from one system to another

Interdisciplinary Concepts
• Heritage
• Citizenship
• Structures

DO
Interdisciplinary Skills
• Problem solving
• Design and construction skills
• Research skills
• Presentation skills
• Interpersonal skills

Topic—Medieval Times
Conceptual Theme—Culture and Change: Then and Now

consist of both topic questions and broader essential questions, and they lead to the enduring understandings. The following are some possible questions for this unit:

• Why are people today still interested in medieval times?

• How did people live in medieval times?

• How do pulleys and gears work, and how did the people use them in medieval times?

• How do the important events of medieval times affect our culture today?

Step 7. Generate instructional activities and assessments aligned with the

KNOW/DO/BE bridge and the culminating assessment. Creating the learning experiences is the final step in the process. If the unit is short, it may involve only one set of learning experiences. If it is a long unit, then teachers should cluster the learning experiences into meaningful mini-units. Guiding questions, natural connections, disciplines, and time limitations influence decisions about which mini-units to teach and how many to teach.

(a) Recluster standards to create mini-units. At this point, teachers may find it helpful to create another web to reconfigure the standards into meaningful chunks rather than into disciplines. These chunks become the mini-units. Teachers can easily

find a natural fit with the broad-based skills and the content in different subject areas. A natural fit, for example, is to teach communication skills in any subject area. Students need good communication skills to communicate (demonstrate) achievement of the standards. Other examples of interdisciplinary skills that offer natural fits are data management and probability skills. These fit well when students do surveys in areas such as social studies. Figure 6.6 is a generic web for the reclustering process. Figure 6.7 shows the web we developed as we brainstormed for possible mini-units for Medieval Times.

(b) Create standards-based learning experiences with built-in assessment. We created three mini-units based on the web we developed. As we designed each activity in each mini-unit, we also considered assessment. In addition, we continually referred to the KNOW/DO/BE, the culminating activity, and the guiding questions to check for alignment. Figure 6.8 shows the organizer we used.

The interdisciplinary curriculum template shown in Figure 6.9 illustrates how the various parts of the process relate to one another. Figure 6.10 provides a checklist that covers all the steps in the design process.

Chapter 7 provides a narrative account of the creation of the interdisciplinary unit on Medieval Times. See also Appendix A for the completed template for the unit.

6.6 Web for Reclustering Content into Mini-Units

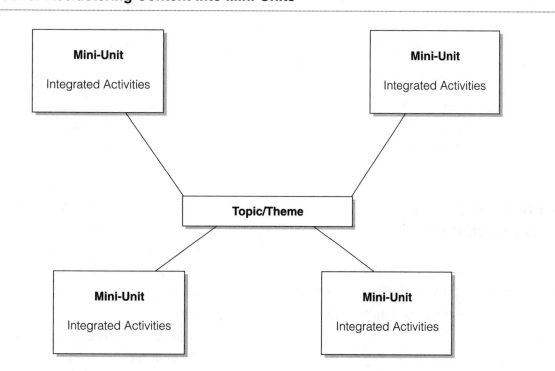

6.7 Mini-Unit Web for Medieval Times

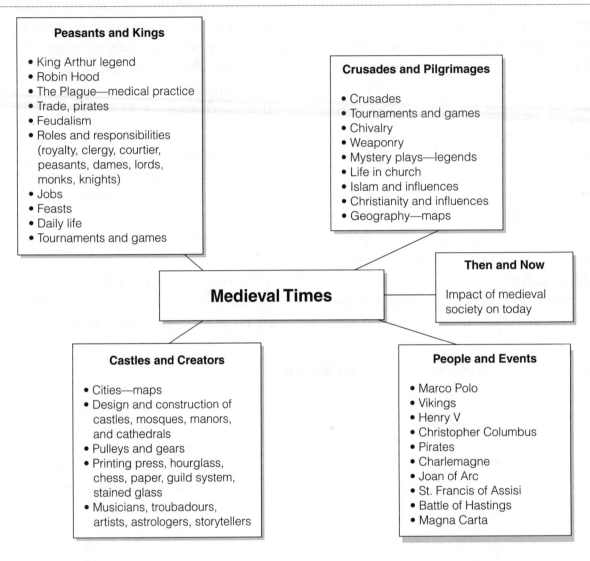

Peasants and Kings

- King Arthur legend
- Robin Hood
- The Plague—medical practice
- Trade, pirates
- Feudalism
- Roles and responsibilities (royalty, clergy, courtier, peasants, dames, lords, monks, knights)
- Jobs
- Feasts
- Daily life
- Tournaments and games

Crusades and Pilgrimages

- Crusades
- Tournaments and games
- Chivalry
- Weaponry
- Mystery plays—legends
- Life in church
- Islam and influences
- Christianity and influences
- Geography—maps

Medieval Times

Then and Now

Impact of medieval society on today

Castles and Creators

- Cities—maps
- Design and construction of castles, mosques, manors, and cathedrals
- Pulleys and gears
- Printing press, hourglass, chess, paper, guild system, stained glass
- Musicians, troubadours, artists, astrologers, storytellers

People and Events

- Marco Polo
- Vikings
- Henry V
- Christopher Columbus
- Pirates
- Charlemagne
- Joan of Arc
- St. Francis of Assisi
- Battle of Hastings
- Magna Carta

Reflections After Implementation

After teaching a unit, teachers need to reflect on its effectiveness. Consider using some of the following questions to guide reflection:

- Did student products/performances reflect mastery of the KNOW/DO/BE?
- Were the teaching activities effective for teaching specific standards to different types of learners? Why or why not?
- Were the assessments appropriate for the activities?

Figure 6.8 Organizer for Teaching, Learning, and Assessing Activities

Mini-Unit Topic: _____

Teaching and Learning Experiences	Standards	Assessment

- Was the BE reflected in student actions?
- What was the student response to the unit? What revisions might be necessary?

- What can we do differently the next time to improve the curriculum design?

6.9 The Interdisciplinary Curriculum Design Template

1. Scan and cluster standards vertically and horizontally to select one or two broad-based standards for each discipline.

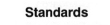

Standards

2. Choose an age-appropriate and relevant topic/theme.

Topic/Theme

3. Create a web to identify potential clusters of standards/content.

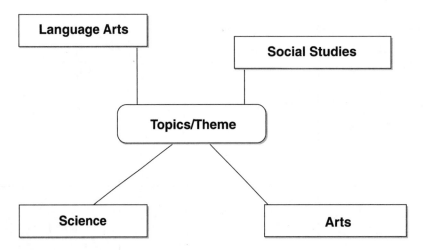

Language Arts

Social Studies

Topics/Theme

Science

Arts

4. Construct a KNOW/DO/BE bridge.

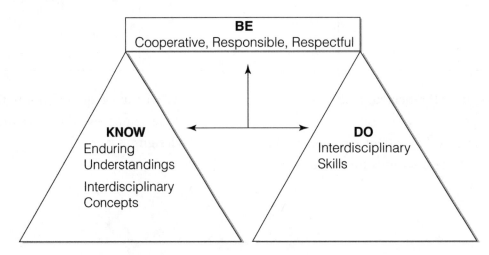

BE
Cooperative, Responsible, Respectful

KNOW
Enduring
Understandings

Interdisciplinary
Concepts

DO
Interdisciplinary
Skills

6.9 The Interdisciplinary Curriculum Design Template (*continued*)

5. Design a culminating assessment.

Assessment task

6. Create guiding questions.

Guiding questions

7. Generate instructional activities and assessments aligned with the KNOW/DO/BE bridge and the culminating assessment:

(a) Recluster standards to develop mini-units.

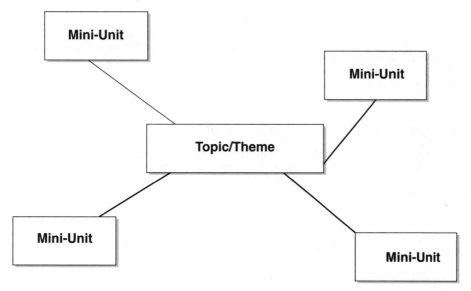

(b) Create standards-based learning experiences with built-in assessment.

Mini-Unit Topic		
Teaching/learning experiences	**Standards**	**Assessment**

6.10 Checklist for Creating an Interdisciplinary Unit

Scan and cluster.

- Did you scan and cluster the curriculum horizontally to identify interdisciplinary concepts and skills?
- Did you scan and cluster the curriculum vertically to establish continuity?
- Did you identify common broad-based standards to act as the foundation for your curriculum unit?

Choose a topic/theme.

Is the identified theme age-appropriate and relevant to students?

Create a web of potential clusters of standards.

Have you brainstormed around the standards to discover a number of possible connections?

Construct the KNOW/DO/BE bridge.

Did you identify the

- KNOW (enduring understandings, transferable concepts, conceptual focus/theme)?
- DO (interdisciplinary skills such as presentation, design and construction, or scientific investigation)?
- BE ("habits of mind" such as respect, teamwork, citizenship)?

Create a culminating assessment.

Does the assessment

- Reflect the KNOW, DO, and BE identified in the learning bridge?
- Provide a way to celebrate learning?
- Clearly identify what students are to do (e.g., rubrics are shared in advance)?
- Require an external audience to witness assess the performance/demonstration?

Create guiding questions.

Do questions

- Provide a framework for the unit?
- Include topic and essential questions?
- Encourage inquiry and multiple answers?
- Encompass a substantial part of the unit?
- Connect to student interests?

Have you provided an opportunity for students to participate in developing the questions?

Generate instructional activities and assessments that align with the KNOW/DO/BE bridge.

- Did you recluster standards to create relevant learning segments?
- Do the activities engage students?
- Are students active learners?
- Is there enough variety and choice in activities to address diverse learning needs?
- Have you addressed the question "How do I know when the student has learned it?" with each activity?
- Does each activity connect to a guiding question?
- Do activities align with the culminating assessment and the KNOW/DO/BE?
- Do performance-based assessments include meaningful and relevant indicators of quality performance?
- Did you share the rubrics with students in advance?
- Do traditional assessments consider the format and skill levels of standardized tests?

7

Castles, Kings . . . and Standards
One Classroom's Experience with Integrated Curriculum

This chapter is adapted from the article "Castles, Kings . . . and Standards," by Susan M. Drake, which appeared in the September 2001 issue of Educational Leadership *(Copyright 2001 by ASCD).*

"How can I create an integrated curriculum when I am locked into covering the standards?" asked Adrian DeTullio, a teacher with three years of experience. Behind DeTullio's question were two assumptions: one, an integrated curriculum leads to more interesting learning experiences; and two, standards constrain teachers to a discipline-based curriculum.

DeTullio teaches 4th grade at St. Ann Catholic School in St. Catharines, Ontario, an affluent community where parents want demonstrable measures of academic success. The school is one of 11 research pilot programs in Ontario studying the effects of parental involvement on school improvement planning. Success on the pilot project will be measured, in part, by results on provincial and school-wide testing.

Unlike some teachers, DeTullio liked the standards because they offered structure. Typically, he would choose one standard from a standards document and plan his lesson around it. Then he would move to the next standard, checking off the standards he had covered. But although he felt accountable, DeTullio was also frustrated. His lessons didn't seem as interesting as they could be.

I teach at the local university and interviewed DeTullio for the research pilot. During the interview, we strayed into my area of interest—integrated curriculum. DeTullio was skeptical that he could teach an integrated curriculum in a test-driven culture. His skepticism echoes that of many educators.

An integrated curriculum enables students to see the big picture, to understand the topic's relevance and real-life context, and to engage in higher-order thinking skills. Some teachers view standards as fragmenting knowledge, impeding instructional flexibility, promoting minimum achievement rather than maximum performance, and failing to lead to higher-order thinking skills (Vars, 2001b). I see an integrated curriculum as the only way to handle the requirements of the standards movement and the knowledge explosion (Drake, 2000).

Could we develop a vibrant curriculum that covered the standards and prepared students for required assessments? DeTullio and I decided to find out. Debra Attenborough, a freelance educator and doctoral student, joined our planning team. Another 4th grade teacher, Dagmar Midgley, implemented the curriculum with DeTullio.

Exploring the Big Picture

The Topic. I asked DeTullio to look through his 4th grade mandated curriculum for possible connections among required units of study. He selected Medieval Times (social studies) and Pulleys and Gears (science and technology). We also added the subjects of language arts and the arts.

The Standards. Our first step was to read all the relevant standards in those subject areas. We looked for standards that were broad-based and cross-disciplinary. Although the content differed by subject area, the skills that students needed were similar. Each document, for example, required research or inquiry skills. We found the following grade 4 standards that promoted research skills:

- Begin to develop research skills (social studies and language arts).
- Formulate questions about and identify needs and problems related to structures and mechanisms in their environment and explore possible solutions and answers (science).
- Solve problems presented through drama and dance and evaluate the effectiveness of each solution (the arts).

The Content. Somewhat embarrassed, we remembered little about the Middle Ages from our school days. We needed a big picture of the content area, so we inquired into other teachers' experiences and surveyed children's books from the school library. DeTullio viewed a CD-ROM and used the Internet. These avenues triggered our memories and offered potential resources for the students.

We felt ready to start.

The Learning Bridge

To help put it together, we wanted a learning bridge to connect the subject areas. The KNOW/DO/BE framework (Drake, 1998) became useful.

The KNOW component includes facts and knowledge—the content. How could we make sense of the content in a meaningful way? Instead of looking at isolated facts, we asked, "What was worth knowing?" For us, the big ideas transcended the specific disciplinary content of a topic. We wanted students to understand concepts and generalizations. These big ideas were not apparent in our standards documents, and we wrestled with what was most important to learn.

The DO component includes skills that students can demonstrate. What was worth doing? For us, students needed broad-based interdisciplinary skills, such as communication, collaboration, information management, and problem solving. These skills transcended any specific content. Students needed to know the content, however, to demonstrate the skills.

The BE area addresses how we want students to be, or how we expect students to act, during the unit. This area was the most important for us, regardless of its relative unimportance in curriculum documents.

With our learning bridge, we were able to structure the Middle Ages unit. The KNOW area dealt with concepts—such as heritage, citizenship, and systems—and generalizations—such as "Citizens have roles and responsibilities," and "Our heritage connects us to the past." The DO area focused on design and construction; research and inquiry; and presentation, both oral and written. The BE area centered around collaboration, responsibility, and respect.

Medieval Times

Early in the process, we realized that a culminating activity would be a good assessment strategy. We would hold a medieval fair in the school gymnasium and invite other classes and parents. We aligned our ideas with the KNOW/DO/BE learning bridge and our overall standards. As we created the daily learning activities, we revisited the culminating activity to ensure that the activities led toward it.

Introductory Activities

Sporting a robe, a gold crown studded in jewels, and a curtain rod as his scepter,

King DeTullio introduced Medieval Times by holding court. He ruled his "subjects" for seven weeks (the crown remained on). His first order was a town meeting to develop a class code of honor, similar to a code of chivalry.

King DeTullio then gave students an overview of the unit. He introduced them to the culminating activity and to ongoing activities, such as diary writing and independent research. He briefly spoke about curriculum integration. Curious, students wondered when, for example, they would do science. "When you make your castles, you will learn about pulleys and gears," he explained. Occasionally, he let them know when they were integrating the curriculum. For example, when students read about the Magna Carta to find out who signed it, he reminded them, "When you are reading, predicting, and finding the main idea, you are learning language arts."

Mini-Units

What would DeTullio teach between the introduction and the culminating activity? This, the heart of the curriculum, required us to consider several ideas. We needed to make sure that we aligned the mini-units with the KNOW/DO/BE learning bridge and the culminating activity. We wanted to leave room for student negotiation, but we needed some specific activities to ensure that we covered the standards.

In our preplanning, we developed four big questions that related to the topic and that were general and interdisciplinary. But we wanted the students to generate their own guiding questions, so we had them brainstorm. DeTullio was delighted by their ability to generate rich questions and was surprised by how similar their questions were to ours. He categorized their 60 questions into the final four:

- What were the important events and people of the times?
- What things were invented and how were they used?
- How were people similar to and different from us?
- How did people live?

Three mini-units survived the planning phase: Peasants and Kings, Castles and Creators, and Crusades and Pilgrimages. During planning, we kept these questions in mind:

- Are the KNOW/DO/BE bridge and the overall standards addressed?
- Do the activities lead to the culminating activity?
- Are we assessing the learning appropriately?
- Is the curriculum relevant and interesting?

Seeing the standards as interconnected eased our task. The standards gave us a chronological order. For example, in Pulleys and Gears, students must observe or describe how pulley and gear systems function, how rotary motion transfers to rotary motion in another system, and how gears operate in one plane and two planes. We followed this set of activities by making a pulley system. The eight standards that related to this performance demonstration were fundamental to research, design, and construction.

The standards for the Pulleys and Gears unit fit perfectly in the mini-unit on Castles and Creators, in which students would be creating a portcullis or drawbridge. DeTullio had previously taught this material one standard at a time, but now it became a seamless process.

We covered language arts and the arts by asking students to demonstrate their learning. Students designed and constructed a castle, wrote research reports and stories, danced, drew portraits, role-played, and gave oral reports. They also read age-appropriate literature. We explicitly taught and evaluated the skills for each activity.

After creating each activity, we recorded the appropriate standards from the relevant subject areas. We covered many more standards than we expected because specific standards folded into broader ones. Recording which standards we were covering gave us a clear picture of what skills and content we explicitly needed to teach and assess.

How did we make the curriculum interesting? Including the arts standards inspired innovation. Resource books and teacher collaboration motivated us. We chose strategies that were hands-on, offered variety, applied to a real-life context, and promoted critical thinking.

Evaluation

The medieval fair was a great success for both students and teachers. The students dressed in medieval garb and decorated the gymnasium with artwork and research materials. Students from other classrooms, teachers, and some parents visited the fair to enjoy the storytelling and dancing.

We had an ongoing dialogue about what to evaluate and how. Students were undergoing schoolwide assessment for basic skills independent of the unit. How much evaluation was enough? We planned for both ongoing and summative assessment.

Referring back to the KNOW/DO/BE bridge, we decided that students could demonstrate their understanding of concepts (KNOW) in their application (DO). But we needed a solid set of rubrics to assess the applications. DeTullio and Midgley evaluated a range of approaches. Synthesizing the mandated curriculum documents, DeTullio developed a chart to show that the standards in all four subject areas focused on reasoning, inquiry, communication, and application. He then developed rubrics, incorporating student input.

How did we separate subjects on report cards? The standards guided us once again. Although we presented the curriculum as a whole, we also addressed each subject area through the subject-specific standards that we had identified in each activity.

Meeting the Unexpected

Finding time was our greatest challenge. Juggling schedules to plan meetings, for example, was difficult. Time also affected implementation. DeTullio and Midgley found that they couldn't complete the entire planned curriculum—the first mini-unit took more than four of the seven weeks. In deciding what to cut, the planning team reviewed the KNOW/DO/BE bridge and the culminating activity.

Another challenge was to cover all the standards. We often went over the list of standards and looked for areas that we had missed. For example, one standard that we had not covered was "to know environmental causes of pollution then and now." We planned to add this explicitly as a category in students' research questions. But this addition was an unnecessary safeguard because the students as researchers selected pollution as crucial to understanding everyday life in medieval culture.

DeTullio commented that, in hindsight, any standard that did not fit into a broader idea did not seem vital to the curriculum. He wondered what would have happened if we had worked with different content. "Does it always work so easily?" he asked. We all agreed that the answer was yes—given careful planning and good content areas.

Did we cover the standards? We checked which standards we had covered after implementing the Peasants and Kings mini-unit. Students brainstormed research questions, completed the research, presented the research in chart form, and held a mock interview. They also created a dance, drew a portrait of a knight, wrote in their ongoing medieval diaries, and read fiction.

We listed all the required standards and checked off those we had authentically covered. We covered a number beyond our expectations: writing, 16 of 25 standards; reading, 19 of 25 standards; oral, 12 of 18 standards; drama and dance, 17 of 21 standards; visual arts, 9 of 17 standards; and social studies, 19 of 21 standards.

There were other surprises. During implementation, we found natural connections with math and realized that we could have legitimately included math in the unit. Students also insisted that we add physical education, and they created medieval dances and played Capture the Flag.

Student Response

How did students do academically? They fared very well on the provincial and board-wide testing. On the teacher-created rubrics, students generally maintained a level 3 (a high level of achievement), with some achieving a level 4.

The teachers noted that students learned both the content and the skills.

Midgley had worried that students would not be able to connect their individual research piece with the larger picture. Would students who researched lords, for example, understand the lords' role in the feudal system? She was pleased to find that students did make connections.

The teachers were particularly pleased with the BE aspect. For example, a group of boys created and performed a dance. "I was blown away," DeTullio said. "I wouldn't have given them 30 seconds to work together without a problem. They worked together for two entire class periods. And they ended their dance with a group hug!" Observing this group perform, I saw no hint of problem behavior. He attributes this amazing breakthrough to the student-created rubric for group behavior. The students had decided that they wanted their code of honor to be the rubric for group behavior and wrote it in their own language.

After the first mini-unit, I asked the students what they had learned. They offered a long list of concepts and generalizations. They knew about life in medieval times and the differences and similarities between then and now. They were sure that they had developed research skills. Like their teachers, they said that the BE area was important. They learned how to cooperate with others, how to be dependable in a group, how to be loyal to the king, how to solve problems without complaining to the teacher, and "how not to blow my top for every little problem."

For teachers and students, the most common descriptor of the unit was "fun." DeTullio said that one of the biggest problems "was keeping the excitement down." Although some students had reservations—one found integration "too confusing"—most said that integration helped them learn better.

The project falls in line with the general research on integrated curriculum. In classes with an interdisciplinary approach, students enjoy the curriculum presentation and achieve positive results (Drake, 2000). And students who learn through an integrated curriculum do as well as, or better than, those who learn through more traditional approaches (Vars, 2000).

Reflections

Excited, DeTullio said that he is "more reflective than before—during and after classroom teaching." Early planning helped, giving him time to understand the big picture. "We taught this unit before and even did some of the same activities, but this year was different." Now he sees the connections across subject areas and across the standards.

Previously, his assessments related only to knowledge and facts. Now he includes higher-order thinking skills. Understanding concepts means being able to demonstrate knowledge through application. Process and content are equally important. Even

DeTullio's teaching style has shifted: "My teacher-centered lessons aren't good enough anymore; I see myself as a facilitator."

A significant factor for success was the collaborative team effort. The team environment encouraged him to continue and helped trigger ideas. More than once, we left a planning session proclaiming, "That was fun!" Equally significant was the collaborative partnership between DeTullio and Midgley. They had worked as a team on other teaching assignments, but veteran teacher Midgley appreciated DeTullio for his new ideas and for making her think. DeTullio learned from her expertise, high expectations, and efficiency. They discussed issues together and made sense of integration.

"Can I create an integrated curriculum when I am locked into covering the standards?" After this unit, DeTullio could answer his own question. Yes, he could develop a vibrant, integrated curriculum that covered the standards. And, given his students' enthusiasm and success, he knew that the project was worth the effort.

8 | Making Connections
A Multidisciplinary Model

For most educators in North America, the years from 1998 to 2002 marked a five-year period of drought for integrated curriculum efforts. Yet, it was exactly during this time that an ambitious five-year project called "Making Connections" flourished in Michigan. What was so special about Making Connections that it was able to transcend the obstacles that had stopped so many other worthy efforts?

Susan learned about Making Connections by attending a workshop sponsored by the school district in Greenville, Michigan. She first visited the LEAP (Learning Through Exploration, Application, and Problem Solving) Center—a multiage program for grades 6 through 8—in the school across the street. The LEAP teachers— Carolyn Slocum, Doug Dodd, Capalene Howse, and Emily Mason— had received training in Making Connections. They used this model for integrating the curriculum in their new program. They recommended that Susan go to one of the training programs so that she could understand the scope of the project beyond the LEAP Center.

In the regional workshop Susan attended, about 60 teachers, grouped into teams from different schools, worked together throughout the day. Connie Riopelle, a consultant, led the workshop with obvious expertise and enthusiasm for integrated approaches. Each team worked with a mentor from the community who facilitated the conversations that occurred in and between small groups. Connie presented recent research indicating the positive results of schools involved in Making Connections during the previous five years. Teams then shared their current progress in creating and implementing integrated curriculum. An excited buzz filled the room. The agenda turned to brain-based learning and ways to apply these concepts to the units of study. Then teams looked at assessment issues and shared, critiqued, and revised rubrics. Finally, they developed or completed plans for action research.

The program was a partnership between the DaimlerChrysler Corporation and the Michigan Department of Education (Michigan Office of Career and Technological Education). Led by Dixie Hibner, the project trained and supported nearly 1,000 teachers from 200 schools in approximately 70 school districts. A talented statewide project team helped prepare and support teaching teams at K–12 schools through extensive training and internal and external coaching. Project leaders encouraged the teams to assess their efforts with ongoing action research. The primary goal of the project was to develop curriculum integration experiences for all students that used rigorous standards and connected to the students' career interests. A second goal was to create partnerships or mentor

relationships with a local business for each school project. The Web site for the California Institute on Human Resources provides details of the project (see http://www.chis.Sonoma.edu and follow the links to Making Connections).

The program evolved from the work of Kathleen Harris of Sonoma University (http://www.harris-consulting.com). Harris, who has worked with more than 5,000 teachers in 42 states, makes no secret of her philosophy for success. For her, both accountability and relevance for students are central to the process. You cannot have one without the other. She has built a unique model that successfully bridges accountability and relevance.

Key Pieces of Making Connections

Making Connections is a multidisciplinary program that culminates in a project that blurs the lines between content areas. Teachers embed essential standards from all disciplines into the project. They use authentic integrated assessment to measure the achievement of all targeted standards. Harris has three key practices that define the Making Connections process: using standards, creating authentic activities, and personalizing the learning to students' strengths.

Using Standards

Making Connections begins with individuals from different subject areas working collaboratively to find a common goal using the standards. Figure 8.1 is the template for the Making Connections process.

Accompanying the template are the following instructions:

1. Identify essential standards in each content area and cross-curricular standards. Each teacher's task, within the team, is to identify the essential standards and levels of performance in the particular area for which he or she is responsible.

2. Determine the common concepts within the standards cited in Step 1. The team must reach agreement about some common ideas across the sets of standards. Select the common concept or theme that the team will use as the basis of the unit/project.

3. Cite the standards that align with the common concept or theme. These targeted standards become the foundation for the unit or project. Team members assume the responsibility for ensuring that they embed their content area and/or cross-curricular standards in an authentic activity.

4. Determine the representative task and assessment for each targeted standard. This will answer the question of what the students need to know and be able to do in order to demonstrate that they have learned the standard.

5. Blend the representative tasks into an integrated activity/unit/project. This will culminate in a product, service, performance, or some combination of these. The integrated activity becomes the vehicle through which the teachers deliver instruction and assess learning.

6. Apply an interest lens to the unit or project to create the contextual learning and career focal point. This allows students to view the unit from their own area of interest. It does not alter the products, services, or performances.

7. Design assessment tools to ensure that students have learned all essential standards. Authentic assessments are critical to determine student learning.

Harris noted that Step 2, determining the common concepts, involves a lot of preparation. Too often teachers accept the first concept they think of without really putting much thought into it. To circumvent this, teachers need to consider concepts in the light of the content, content standards, and cross-curricular standards (skills). Teachers receive materials such as the SCANS chart (see Chapter 3 and Figure 3.11), the Michigan Curricular Framework, and the Missouri Show Me Standards. These materials offer different versions of broad-based skills or cross-curricular standards (skills). The Making Connections process uses many of the principles described in Chapter 4.

Creating Authentic Activities

Harris has woven together brain research theory, constructivist theory, and

8.1 Making Connections Template

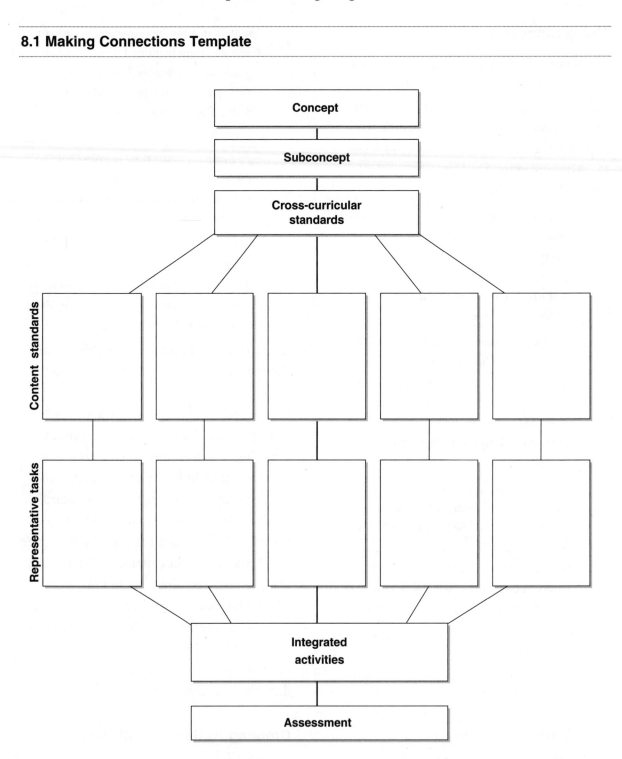

Source: Kathleen Harris, California Institute on Human Services, Sonoma State University, Rohnert Park, California.

multiple intelligences theory to help teachers understand why and how to create the most effective instructional activities. She recommends authentic, integrated activities that connect to the real world—usually the world of work. A real-world problem often provides the foundation for learning activities. In addition, teachers need to allow for multiple ways of learning.

Authentic activities streamline assessment. For example, rather than write a test to demonstrate mastery of new vocabulary, teachers may assess student understanding by their use of appropriate vocabulary in the context of an integrated activity. At Lansing High School in Lansing, Michigan, Ernest Estrada, the 9th grade team leader, works with world geography teacher June DeBois, science teacher Stephanie Robinson, English teacher Christie McGonical, and administrator Gwendolyn Bodiford. They have found that streamlining assessment with the activities gives them much more time for teaching. A constant question for them is, "What do kids have to do to tell us that they know it?" When students demonstrate what they know and can do through a performance, the need for written testing is much less. The activity *is* the assessment.

Some of the 9th grade students at East Bay High School in Gibsonton, Florida, are enrolled in an aquaculture program. To create an integrated activity that was authentic and reflected a real-world problem, teachers looked to their community. The

curriculum planners were Michael Yates (lead teacher, Aquaculture Academy), Charlotte Hughes (coordinator of grants and projects, Technical and Career Education, School District of Hillsborough County, Florida), assistant principal Sharon Morris, social studies teacher John Sporandio, and reading teacher Diane Roberson. They set up the scenario found in Figure 8.2. The curriculum plan they devised is described later in this chapter.

Personalizing the Learning

Harris is a strong believer in integrated curriculum and authentic assessment. Her vast experience with all varieties of learners—particularly those at risk—has taught her, however, that this approach is not enough in itself. A student needs to be intrinsically motivated to learn.

Harris relates a dramatic incident of how she came to this "aha." Visiting a physics class, she witnessed a cooperative group activity designed to teach the concept of distribution of weight. All groups received a box of similar supplies. Circles of identical size were drawn on the floor. The task was to build a structure from outside the circle that would hold up a heavy weight. Harris noted that a certain type of student thrived on this task. Other types of students distanced themselves from the activity. Intuitively, she understood that if she could provide personal meaning for the activity, she could draw in other students. She changed the instructions. A child was stuck

8.2 A Real-World Problem Used in the Making Connections Program

You are a consultant for East Bay Aquaculture Consulting (EBAC). You have been hired by Steve Lapia to evaluate and make recommendations to him to address his regulatory problems. Mr. Lapia owns and operates a 20-acre fish farm in Wimauma. His farmland lies adjacent to Wimauma Woods, a new residential development owned by Wimauma Woods Corporation. The corporation is attempting to force Mr. Lapia out of business for noncompliance with environmental regulations. He realizes he may indeed be out of compliance with the Florida Department of Agriculture and Consumer Services Division of Aquaculture and needs advice.

On a fact-finding visit to the T. Lapia Farm, the following observations and facts were gathered:

- Mr. Lapia's property abuts a beautiful large lake. He has operated the fish farm for 12 years. He raises Danios, Kissers, and Gromies. His production system includes a combination of above-ground standing vats housed in greenhouse structures and more than 40 dirt-water ponds. A variety of tropical fish thrive in the drainage ditches on his property.
- Mr. Lapia has two employees who are paid $4.25 per hour. Mr. Lapia allows them to work in shorts, barefooted, and without shirts. Fish medications are stored on open shelves. His employees handle medications without gloves.
- The production system generators and the whole electrical system have no breakers and no ground fault interrupts (GFIs), and the electrical wiring runs from receptacle to receptacle without enclosed conduit cases.
- Mr. Lapia sorts and grades the fish out by the pond. If a fish does not meet the order grade (size and coloring), he and his employees dump the nongrade fish on the ground (a process called "culling the fish").
- Mr. Lapia has a producer permit that is up to date. He has collected several dozen freshwater flounder and has them in a large greenhouse vat.
- He has had problems with otters and has put out poison. He also has a problem with birds stealing fish out of his open-dirt ponds and often shoots at the birds.

As a consultant, you will do the following:

- Research appropriate regulatory agencies (refer to best practices Aquaculture Module).
- Identify whether the agencies involved are federal, state, or local.
- Gather and note citation information for regulations (noncompliance items) by agency applicable to Mr. Lapia's farm.
- Develop a list of noncompliance items along with appropriate regulations including documentation.
- Write an outline for a recommendation report for Mr. Lapia.
- Write a final recommendation report.

Source: Michael Yates, Charlotte Hughes, Sharon Morris, John Sporandio, and Diane Roberson, East Bay High School, Gibsonton, Florida.

in a well with his arms wedged against the sides. What if students had the same box of tools and had to build a structure to get the child out? The group that Harris had been observing became quickly engrossed in the task. They designed a pulley and a counterweight to solve the problem. As well, they went beyond the initial problem and learned new concepts about relevant health issues, such as changes in blood gases as related to anoxia and loss of consciousness. The physics teacher noted that this was the first time that the group had really been involved in a physics activity.

Once teachers design a standards-driven authentic activity, they need to search for ways to make it personally meaningful to the learner. Harris has developed a motivation preference model that builds on the theories of multiple intelligences and temperament sorters. The model seeks to identify intrinsic or natural motivators rather than personality traits. It categorizes student interests in four quadrants: People and Relationships, Things and Functions, Discovery and Processes, and Creativity and Expression (see Figure 8.3). Matching a student's motivational preference to an instructional activity is a part of curriculum design. The students who appreciated the physics teacher's take on building a structure fell into the Things and Functions quadrant. Those who were motivated by the child-trapped-in-a-well scenario were in the People and Relationships quadrant.

The motivation preference system goes beyond learning styles to ask, "What natural incentives can I use to motivate student interests?" Harris found that when teachers changed what they did to match learning styles, the standards got lost in the process. However, by focusing on motivational preferences, teachers also can concentrate on standards. Once teachers create an authentic activity, they must view it through a motivational lens. Does the activity motivate students? Harris has typically worked with high-risk students who need to be motivated intrinsically. Sometimes a different scenario will capture students' attention. At other times, for example, different focus questions or presenting to different audiences can act as motivational lenses.

The shifts that teachers make by using the motivation preferences chart can be subtle but powerful. For example, a 5th grade class was doing a unit on Explorers and Cartography that integrated language arts, personal studies, art, and music. The teachers asked students to complete a map of the explorer's expedition and to give a presentation. The presentation included why the expedition was important, a portrait of the explorer, and a piece of music representative of where the explorer had been. The activities were not capturing student interest. The teachers applied the motivational preference lens and changed the task. Students adopted the role of a fictional character on the expedition. One student, for example, became a Native American medicine man. Students

8.3 Motivation Preference

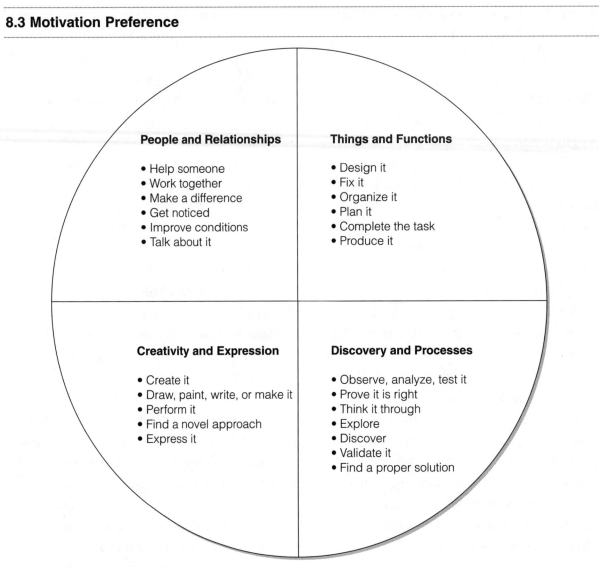

People and Relationships

- Help someone
- Work together
- Make a difference
- Get noticed
- Improve conditions
- Talk about it

Things and Functions

- Design it
- Fix it
- Organize it
- Plan it
- Complete the task
- Produce it

Creativity and Expression

- Create it
- Draw, paint, write, or make it
- Perform it
- Find a novel approach
- Express it

Discovery and Processes

- Observe, analyze, test it
- Prove it is right
- Think it through
- Explore
- Discover
- Validate it
- Find a proper solution

Source: Kathleen Harris Consulting Inc.

now wrote journals from the perspective of the fictional character. Interest escalated once students actually put themselves into the expedition.

Harris notes that teachers should merge as many activities as possible into authentic work. However, sometimes the need to teach and to assess a specific standard dic-tates the learning activities and makes them difficult to integrate into an authentic activity. In this case, she recommends working with students to change their perspective on this type of necessary, but nonauthentic, activity.

The motivational preference model works for curriculum planning teams, too.

Harris finds that teachers working together are very good at designing interesting and challenging activities that cover the standards. Often teachers who choose to work together fall naturally into the four quadrants. Thus, they create activities in all four motivational preference categories. Once teachers are familiar with the motivational preference tool, they use it explicitly to appeal to students' strengths. They make sure that they include activities for the different types of learners in their classrooms.

Applying the Making Connections Template

For an example of how teachers have successfully used Making Connections, let's return to the team from East Bay High School in Gibsonton, Florida, that applied the template to the real-world problem presented in Figure 8.2. The students targeted for this curriculum were in an aquaculture program that they had selected because they had an interest in this area. The teachers assumed, therefore, that the activity would motivate the students. They created a lesson titled "Wimauma Woods Versus Steve T. Lapia." They organized their curriculum plan around the concept regulations and the subconcept aquaculture business regulations in Florida.

They identified a number of cross-curricular standards in the subject areas

of American government, aquaculture foundations, and language arts. Then they devised various representative tasks, such as "Identify specific government regulatory role," "Apply regulations in the identification of noncompliance issues to a specific business profile," and "Read and summarize regulatory documents." The integrated activities that the students undertook required them to take on the role of a business consultant to the aquatic business owner. They were expected to research and become familiar with pertinent state regulations, apply them to the situation in the scenario, and prepare a regulation compliance/noncompliance report for the business owner. To assess student performance, teachers evaluated the consultant reports using an established rubric. (See Appendix B for the complete template the teachers developed for this unit and the rubric they used.)

Research

The final report on the Michigan project (Warner & Heinz, 2002) provides a good sense of the effectiveness of the Making Connections approach. In the first two years of the program, the Michigan State Department commissioned a study with 45 of the schools involved in Making Connections to determine the levels of implementation. Researchers collected data on eight "key elements of high-quality integrated programs" as identified by Harris:

- The program targets student interests.
- Standards help to establish connections and concepts.
- Coursework is inquiry-based and student-centered.
- Assessment involves significant thinking and complex activities.
- Instructional teams and student groups have a clear identity within the institution.
- Institutional teams have resources and authority to make decisions about their programs.
- Industry, business, parents, and community agencies are involved and supportive.
- Community-based learning is central to the program.

Results showed that the programs had a high degree of implementation. A survey completed by participants at the end of 2001 indicated that 80 percent of them expressed excitement about their participation. More than 60 percent said they would continue to implement Making Connections because it increased student interest (45 percent), student learning (38 percent), administrative support (38 percent), and career focus of students (33 percent).

From 2001 to 2002, 20 teams from 13 schools in nine Michigan school districts conducted action research. Each team in the study developed a hypothesis based on one or more of the eight key elements and its relationship to student achievement, attendance, retention, and discipline. Teams reported very positive results:

- The students at Making Connections sites did at least as well as, if not better than, they had done previously in achievement, attendance, retention, and discipline measures.
- All teams that reported on achievement and discipline reported improvement.
- Among the 11 teams tracking attendance, 10 reported improved attendance and 1 reported little change.

Sandy Jeannotte is the director of curriculum for the Cheboygan Area School District in Cheboygan, Michigan. The Making Connections work done in her area demonstrates the power and potential of the program. For Jeannotte, "the Making Connections project has profoundly changed how we align, write, and teach the assigned curriculum." From 1998 to 2002, 16 Cheboygan K–12 schools were involved in the project. One of the best indicators of the success of Making Connections is the performance of the Cheboygan Area School District graduating class of 2002. These students, who had been in the program since it began in the 1996–97 school year, showed dramatic increases in their scores on the Michigan Education Assessment Program (MEAP).

Why It Works

The assumptions embedded in Harris's model are revealing:

- The key to success is the focus on standards without dismissing the importance of personal meaning.
- Teachers achieve relevance through tuning into what naturally motivates a particular student to learn.
- All students can learn if they have the right motivation.

- Teachers can mold a standards-based curriculum to accommodate motivational preferences.
- Authentic tasks and assessments offer the greatest potential for motivation.
- Teachers who work collaboratively can and do create curriculum that is both motivating and relevant.

Clearly, the Making Connections model offers a great deal for thoughtful educators to consider.

9

A Mission to Transform Education

Newsome Park Elementary School

One can start with almost any object or idea and, through questioning, reflecting, and imagining, see through it like a window into the depth and breadth of the world.

—Steven Levy, *Starting from Scratch* (1996), p. xvi.

On a warm, sunny day in May, Rebecca visited Newsome Park Elementary School in Newport News, Virginia. The hallways were galleries of learning, with displays of student projects flanking classroom doors on both sides. Some students, visibly anticipating the opportunity to share their learning with adults, were putting final touches on the class displays. Others were greeting visitors and directing them to the displays. Many students were in their classrooms engaged in learning activities but eagerly anticipating their turn to tell the visitors what they had learned. It was Exhibition Day for the second-semester projects!

For students at Newsome Park, Exhibition Day occurs twice each year—in January and May. On Exhibition Day, students display the quality products that result from their investigations of problems and issues that directly affect them and their community.

A kindergarten child tugged at Rebecca's sleeve and asked her to come over and see what he had learned in a class project about working dogs. Rebecca stood mesmerized as she watched this 6-year-old operate a wireless computer that displayed pictures and descriptions of various dogs. Alongside the computer were racks of books the students had used in their investigation along with the computer. Then the little boy and his partner began to explain what would happen if there were no working dogs, what impact the dogs have on the community, and what humans can do for these hard-working animals—"big" questions that students had answered through the project. Rebecca was especially interested to learn that the class had worked with the local Society for the Prevention of Cruelty to Animals to organize a donation of dry cat and dog food, dog treats, and newspapers. This added a service-learning component to the project and benefited the community.

Obviously, the students had learned a great deal about working dogs. Nevertheless, how did this project connect to the Standards of Learning (SOLs) that students must master? As she checked the display more closely, Rebecca found a list of all SOLs addressed. The list included six English standards related to oral language, reading comprehension, and writing; seven in math related to computation and estimation, geometry, probability and statistics, patterns, functions, and algebra; two in social studies related to economics; and four

in science related to scientific investigation, matter, and resources.

As Rebecca visited all the class displays, she found evidence of student engagement, excitement, and learning. Students proudly shared what they had learned about their "big questions" and adeptly answered other questions that she posed about their learning. Every project displayed student findings, community connections, and alignment to the standards.

Transformation at Newsome Park

Since 1995, administrators, teachers, and students at Newsome Park have been actively engaged in a mission to transform education through project-based learning. The school's Web site contains a wealth of information about Newsome Park and its instructional program (http://npes.nn.k12 .va.us). The school's mission statement, posted on their Web site, guides their efforts:

> The students at Newsome Park Elementary are actively engaged in a child-centered learning environment. The faculty and staff provide knowledge work, which is meaningful to the learners and their community. The students are expected to solve problems and produce quality products that will enable them to increase their competencies to continue learning independently.

Newsome Park Elementary is a K–5 math, science, and technology magnet school that serves approximately 750 students from across the Newport News district. Children work in heterogeneous classes, and they remain with the same teachers for two years: K–1, 2–3, and 4–5. Students who enroll enjoy special experiences and opportunities in math, science, and technology while gaining a solid foundation in language arts, history and social science, the arts, and physical education. Teachers integrate technology across all content areas. Students use technology to gather, analyze, and communicate information. They also make decisions about what forms of technology they use to demonstrate and reinforce learning.

Although teachers at Newsome Park were using an integrated thematic approach to curriculum, students did not have a voice in deciding what the themes would be, and student performance on standardized tests was poor. After initiating project-based learning, students began doing better on the tests. Principal Peter Bender attributes the gains to the fact that project-based learning begins with student questions. He says the students feel ownership of a project and are committed to investigating it because the questions have meaning for them. Students are engaged in planning project activities, and they feel they can make an impact by answering the questions or solving the problem.

Daily and weekly schedules for teachers and students support project-based learning by providing time for planning, implementation, and evaluation of projects. Peter

Bender and his teachers meet every Wednesday afternoon for common planning time. Children come early four mornings each week, and they leave at 12:30 on Wednesday to allow for the planning time. In addition to planning, teachers and principal use the time to review projects and to double-check that each project addresses the state standards. Student success at Newsome Park is the obvious result of effective planning, instruction, and program evaluation.

Teachers at Newsome Park believe strongly in a constructivist approach to teaching and learning. They believe that people learn by actively constructing knowledge, weighing new information against previous knowledge, thinking about and working through discrepancies, and eventually reaching a new understanding. This is evident in the project approach as well as the school's emphasis on character education, technology, and service learning. In the classrooms at Newsome Park, students explore phenomena or ideas. They question, create, and share hypotheses with others, revise their thinking, and present their learning.

Phases in Project Development

Project-based learning seeks to blend authentic, real-world experiences with rigorous academic study. Projects, which usually are cross-disciplinary, engage students in activities that are interesting to them and important to the course of study. Projects may involve community members and settings, and they often result in an exhibition or product for an audience.

Teachers and students conceive, implement, and assess projects through a three-phase process based on the work of Sylvia Chard (1998). Phase 1 is for planning; Phase 2 is for fieldwork; Phase 3 is for sharing the learning.

Phase 1: Preparation or Incubation

The first phase of project development involves students in obtaining information and processing it internally. This phase includes four activities:

- Defining prior knowledge
- Representing the knowledge through pictures, drawings, language, writings, and mathematics
- Defining what is known and raising questions to be answered
- Integrating Virginia SOLs

During Phase 1, students, and sometimes teachers, raise questions or present ideas for a project. Frequently, teachers and students want to connect to a previous project. For example, a project on protection of animals led to another project on hunting domestic versus wild animals. According to Marie Ciafre, a 5th grade teacher, if a teacher has a burning idea for a project, she "plants a seed" by sharing ideas with students, bringing in readings related to the project idea, or creating a classroom environment using materials about the topic that stimulate the students' interest.

Most often, project ideas originate with students. For example, the 2nd grade class embarked on a project about Newsome Park, the area of Newport News for which the school is named. The idea stemmed from a book written by a student. The student turned his book into a slide show to convince his classmates that this would be a good project. He began looking through the standards to see which concepts and skills the class might learn by studying the history of Newsome Park. He recruited two classmates to help him rewrite the standards into student-friendly language. Ultimately, he convinced the class and his teacher that the project was relevant and included accountability for the standards. In all, the project addressed 29 standards in four content areas.

Teachers must ensure that the class projects provide opportunities for meaningful learning experiences that they can integrate across the curriculum. Once that is established, teachers weave different aspects of math, science, reading, and writing into each project, making sure the project addresses the standards.

To complete Phase 1, students generate "big" questions about the topic. The big-question approach (Murphy & Singer, 2001) uses current events to help frame and examine complex and controversial questions about the contemporary world.

More specifically, it engages students in posing and examining questions about the problems facing their communities and the world. Teachers introduce these broad and complex questions repeatedly from different points of view through the curriculum. In the Newsome Park project, questions included the following:

- What was Newsome Park like a long time ago and how has it changed?
- Why does a wheel represent our school?
- How is the school important to the community?

Finally, students brainstorm activities that support the inquiry. Students and teachers complete most of Phase 1 in daily class meetings.

Phase 2: Inspiration/Verification

During Phase 2, students find and evaluate solutions to problems. They participate in the following activities:

- Complete field study and field work
- Learn to represent knowledge as investigations are occurring; use databases, word processing, Internet, spreadsheets, graphs, charts, surveys
- Begin to share knowledge, critique findings, test theories
- Identify additional SOLs

Teachers integrate Phase 2 work into the regular school day. They use a weekly planning tool like that shown in Figure 9.1

to outline the standards, essential understandings, and guiding questions that make up the week's instructional focus. The tool also indicates the evidence teachers use to assess student learning. In addition, it includes ways in which they make connections to the current class project. If a situation arises in which a teacher cannot integrate certain standards into a project, she or he covers them through a mini-project or direct instruction.

Project work extends through the semester, with dates set for exhibitions at the beginning of the semester. The amount of time devoted to project work may vary according to the project's needs.

A project about sickle-cell disease is a good example of Phase 2 work. Spurred by a newspaper article about a classmate with the disease, students visited a local hospital and clinic, read books about hospitals and blood, and conducted a survey of adults and students to determine their attitudes about shots and other medical procedures. In this and other projects, students take their questions to the community.

In Phase 2, teachers and students construct a time line and benchmarks for project completion. Teachers allow students to go in new directions, but guide them and help them stay on course. Because the projects at Newsome Park are class projects, teachers help students learn how to work collaboratively. Teachers designate specific group roles for students and provide guidance on resources. They also create rubrics

9.1 Weekly Curriculum Planning Tool for Project-Based Learning

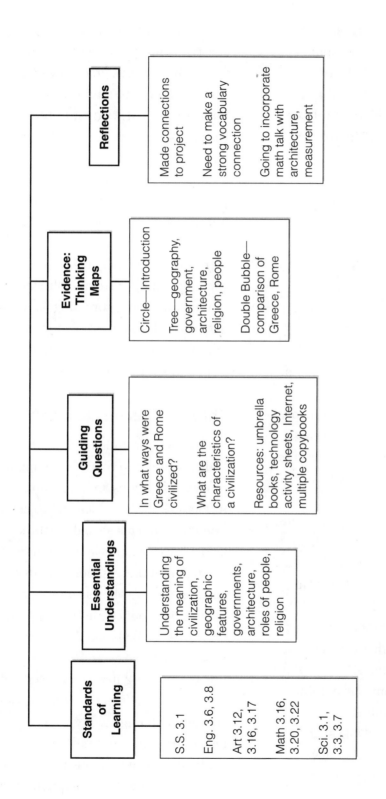

Standards of Learning	Essential Understandings	Guiding Questions	Evidence: Thinking Maps	Reflections
S.S. 3.1 Eng. 3.6, 3.8 Art 3.12, 3.16, 3.17 Math 3.16, 3.20, 3.22 Sci. 3.1, 3.3, 3.7	Understanding the meaning of civilization, geographic features, governments, architecture, roles of people, religion	In what ways were Greece and Rome civilized? What are the characteristics of a civilization? Resources: umbrella books, technology activity sheets, Internet, multiple copybooks	Circle—Introduction Tree—geography, government, architecture, religion, people Double Bubble—comparison of Greece, Rome	Made connections to project Need to make a strong vocabulary connection Going to incorporate math talk with architecture, measurement

Teacher: _____

Week: _____

Source: Principal Peter Bender and the staff at Newsome Park Elementary School, Newport News, Virginia.

for projects that include what is required for the final product and what it should look like. Figure 9.2 is a rubric Marie Ciafre uses in her 5th grade class to assess how well students work collaboratively on a social studies presentation. The rubric includes both teacher assessment and student self-assessment.

Teachers at Newsome Park expect students to work on quality products daily. A product is the ultimate outcome of a project. Marie Ciafre says that teachers must ask, "What are the quality pieces of the final product?" and "Which students will be responsible for each quality piece?"

Students reflect on their learning at the end of each school day, at the completion of a class project, and after sharing their learning with the public. Teachers say this helps build a community of learners. If kids have had a problem working together, the teacher may have them participate in a conflict-resolution activity during this time.

In Phase 2, teachers also integrate commercially available teaching tools with project-based learning. These include Thinking Maps, Write from the Beginning, and Futurekids. Thinking Maps (http://www.thinkingmaps.com) contains various types of conceptual maps that teachers and students use during different phases of the project to conceptualize and clarify thinking about a topic. Write from the Beginning, which is also available at the Thinking Maps Web site, is a K–5 developmental writing program that emphasizes narrative, expository, descriptive, and persuasive writing. Teachers extend instruction from previous grades by using writing rubrics and focused mini-lessons to help improve student writing. Futurekids (http://www.futurekids.com), a program from School Technology Solutions, is designed to help schools integrate the power of technology to facilitate and improve student performance. Teachers create lesson plans with student assignments and rubrics by using computer hardware, operating systems, software evaluation, word processing, spreadsheets, databases, desktop publishing, multimedia, telecommunications, curriculum integration, and application integration.

Phase 3: Communication/Validation

In Phase 3, students share their learning and compare it to others' thinking through project exhibitions and community service. In Phase 3 of the sickle-cell project, for example, students shared what they had learned with parents and community through oral presentations, written reports, and a brochure. They also made a community service connection by preparing posters for a schoolwide blood drive. Phase 3 of a project called From Trash to Treasure involved making items from recycled materials and collecting and recycling cans. In another recycling study, Would Society Benefit from Reusing and Reducing Plastic?, students sent suggestions to the local newspaper, the *Daily Press,* on alternate methods

9.2 Rubric for Collaboration on a Social Studies Presentation

4	3	2	1
Showed respect for the ideas of other members in the group while participating very often.	Showed respect for the ideas of other members in the group while participating often.	Showed respect for the ideas of other members in the group while participating most of the time.	Showed respect for the ideas of other members of the group while participating very little.
Organized information into a tree map using detailed and accurate information under the four "big questions" regarding topic.	Organized information into a tree map using detailed and accurate information under three of the four "big questions."	Organized information into a tree map using detailed and accurate information under two of the four "big questions."	Organized information into a tree map using detailed and accurate information under one of the four "big questions."
Cooperated a lot with other members of the group to create a visual poster displaying pictures representing assigned ancient culture.	Cooperated often with other members of the group to create a visual poster displaying pictures representing assigned ancient culture.	Cooperated most of the time with other members of the group to create a visual poster displaying pictures representing assigned ancient culture.	Cooperated some of the time with other members of the group to create a visual poster displaying pictures representing assigned ancient culture.
Worked a lot with other members of the group to create an artifact representing assigned ancient culture.	Worked often with other members of the group to create an artifact representing the assigned ancient culture.	Worked most of the time with other members of the group to create an artifact representing assigned ancient culture.	Worked some of the time with other members of the group to create an artifact representing assigned ancient culture.
Date:_____	Student: My score _____	Teacher: My score _____	Did we match?_____

Source: Marie Ciafre, Newsome Park Elementary School, Newport News, Virginia.

to deliver their newspapers other than plastic bags. Class members also met with *Daily Press* officials to explain what really happens to the plastic bags even though they are recyclable.

Teacher Reflections

Although project-based learning requires extra time for planning, teachers are enthu-siastic about its benefits. Following are a few of their reflections on the value of project-based learning:

> We had behavioral challenges and wanted to create respect for learners. Using projects, especially with the community service component, helps kids come together for a cause that is not their own. They become more giving.

> We have to trust kids to take a project in their direction.

We value kids as theorists.

Integration (through projects) is the only way you can teach everything that is required.

Student Learning

On Exhibition Day at Newsome Park, excitement runs high. Students often ask visitors to "ask me what I learned." The explanations Rebecca heard on her visit were quite clear and detailed. It was obvious that students had learned a great deal from their projects. Moreover, standardized test scores continue to underscore that students at Newsome Park are mastering the required Standards of Learning. These are some comments students shared about their learning through projects:

> I learned to use different computer functions and programs to draft a letter to city planners.
>
> I learned to skim through material and pick out just the important information.
>
> I learned that if I looked hard enough I would find the information I needed.
>
> Last year all we really did was write down in our notebooks, and that is how we kept up with our information we learned; but now we get to experience and we get to touch more than hear; we can keep it in our brains and, it is, like, stuck.

If the current trend in test performance at Newsome Park continues, students will score at or above Virginia's 70 percent pass-ing requirement in the core areas when they reach 3rd grade. Project-based learning has been the focal point for the curriculum since 1998, and each year since then students' test scores on the Virginia Standards of Learning Test have improved steadily and dramatically. In both 3rd and 5th grades, African American and white students, the two major groups in the school, have shown significant growth. Between 1999 and 2002, the percentage of African American 3rd graders who achieved passing rates increased by 45 percentage points in English, 30 percentage points in math, 51 percentage points in science, and 34 percentage points in history. Passing rates for white students increased by 17 percentage points in English, 8 in math, 8 in science, and 12 in history. These results indicate that the achievement gap between African American and white students also is narrowing—by 28 points in English, 22 in math, 43 in science, and 22 in history. Results for 5th grade students are somewhat less dramatic, but still impressive, with significant gains registered for both black and white students in English, writing, math, and science.

In a school divided almost equally by race, and with 50 percent of its students receiving free or reduced-price lunch, all students are making good progress toward mastering essential concepts and skills. Additional indicators of the success of project-based learning include increased student attendance, decreased discipline referrals and special education referrals, a lower retention rate, and a waiting list for student enrollment.

The staff at Newsome Park Elementary School have truly transformed education for their students.

10 The Alpha Program
Students as Standards-Based Curriculum Designers

It was a bright autumn day when Susan visited the Alpha program in Shelburne, Vermont. This alternative program has operated since 1972 within the more traditional Shelburne Community School, a K–8 school. All 69 of the 6th through 8th grade students in the program sat on the floor for their thematic unit design meeting. They were eagerly awaiting the three presentations of the course of study that they, the students, had developed for the rest of the year. Their teachers, Cynthia Myers, Joan Cavallo, and Meg O'Donnell, were equally excited.

The course of study included three themes that had evolved through a process of generating relevant student questions and closely exploring the mandated state standards. In each presentation, students stated the theme and identified the standards, written in student-friendly language. They described learning experiences with appropriate assessments that would enable them to cover the standards in a relevant way. There was no mention of disciplines.

The students offered positive feedback on the presentations. "I think everyone did a good job." "It was really neat how everyone worked together."

When asked if designing the curriculum had been useful to them, students responded with a resounding and enthusiastic yes. The teachers told them how pleased they were with the student planning; now they could help them arrange for the proposed activities for the whole year.

How can a student-designed curriculum exist in an age of accountability? How do these students manage to do well on state tests when there is no direct teaching to the test? What is the role of the teachers? How do parents respond to such a program? Clearly, the Alpha program is unique and offers many insights for creating a successful interdisciplinary program.

The Evolution of Alpha

The Alpha Team consists of 6th, 7th, and 8th grade students working in partnership with their teachers in an integrated, multiage community. It is one of several middle school programs available at Shelburne Community School. Within the larger school organization, students rank their choices for which program they wish to attend. Alpha teachers prefer to admit those who select the team as their first choice. However, they support the administrative practice of admitting some other students for balance and diversity. Students who arrive in the program as a second or third choice generally become involved quickly

and join in enthusiastically. Alpha has full inclusion of special education students.

Much of the premise for the program comes from James Beane's philosophy (see, for example, *A Middle School Curriculum: From Rhetoric to Reality,* 1990/1993). Beane believes that students learn best when they are engaged in answering their own questions. For him, students do have meaningful questions that generally cover much of the required curriculum when organized into social and personal concerns. The Alpha experience affirms Beane's beliefs. A second key belief guiding the Alpha philosophy is that successful learning needs to occur in a safe place where all children feel that they belong. In this safe environment, teachers and students value academic excellence and encourage individuality and risk taking.

Alpha students learn in three multiage groups. One Alpha teacher guides each group. Large blocks of time and open physical spaces provide for a variety of student groupings and various learning experiences. Each day, all students attend a classroom meeting to discuss what is happening. Here, the weekly schedule appears on the whiteboard; teachers post weekly academic goals in math, reading, writing, spelling, and theme expectations.

The curriculum is standards-based, thematic, and interdisciplinary. Students participate in the Connected Math program separately at specific grade levels. Students also go to "unified arts" (art, physical education, French, and music) for one hour and 20 minutes a day (the teachers use this block of time for common planning). The integrated program evolves from student questions and links to required standards. Here are some examples of past themes:

- In the Beginning: A Study of Origins
- Advocacy: The Power of One (geography)
- We the People (government)
- Nutrition
- Business and Economics
- Culture
- Careers
- Conflict Resolution
- Natural Resources
- Living Systems

Students often work on large projects. A typical project was the development of a company called CLAY-Z during the study of the Business and Economic theme. Students produced, marketed, and sold five different products made from clay: tea-bag holders, soap dishes, coaster sets, handmade boxes, and magnet sets. Students assumed various roles in this project, such as management team, human resource staff, marketers, production workers, or packagers. Two other thematic units appear in detail in *Integrated Studies in the Middle Grades* (Stevenson & Carr, 1993). Adopt a Business was an interdisciplinary study of local businesses. The Big Alpha Circus

included teachers of art, music, and physical education from outside the Alpha unit.

The Alpha philosophy includes the development of a sense of community and leadership. As a result, a number of activities are required throughout the year to support this goal. They include the following:

- Orientation activities and an 8th grade leadership retreat
- Annual play—required participation in after-school practice and evening performances
- Annual family dinner
- Quilt and camping trip
- 8th grade finale
- Culminating events
- Daily morning meetings and student-led class meetings with class officers

Parental Involvement

Parents are involved at many levels, including being partners in the ongoing assessment of their children. They attend culminating events and monthly meetings over dinner. The program has an active parent council. The parent council runs a buddy system for new parents—veteran parents call them to address any questions they might have. In addition, an advocacy group meets regularly with principal John Bossange as a proactive measure.

These parents feel some pressure from others who wonder how Alpha students prepare for higher grades and learn the required knowledge and skills in an environment that does not center on traditional subject classes. Fortunately, recent quantitative data supporting student achievement should reassure them. In addition, the parents reported that students who went on to high school did very well because they had learned how to learn and how to ask good questions. The parents that Susan met clearly believed that Alpha was a great experience for their children. For them, "a successful Alpha parent" is one who asks questions, trusts the teachers, and listens to why and how this type of program works. As one parent said, "We need to be willing to let go of how we learned and think about what is best for the child."

Negotiating the Curriculum

At the beginning of each year, students brainstorm for questions that interest them. They create 10 questions around the area of "self" and 10 questions about "the world." Students then meet in groups to decide which questions will lead to the richest and most relevant study. The students Susan observed asked some frivolous questions, but also some very good ones, such as these:

Self:

- How many times does your heart beat in a lifetime?

- How do genes affect your physical traits?
- Why do people like and dislike different sports?
- Who are my ancestors?
- What can I do to make the world a better place?
- How do you get your personality if it is not in your genes?
- Why do we dream?
- Why do we sleepwalk?
- Why do humans live longer than other species?
- What career will I have?

The World:

- What came first, the chicken or the egg?
- Why do we have "time"?
- Who made up languages? Why do we have them?
- What would it be like to live in the past?
- Why is there poverty?
- Is there such a thing as a parallel universe?
- Why is the world round?
- Why do presidents seem to be more concerned about their reputations than about their country?

Once the small groups generated the questions, it was time to consider possible themes. All 69 students reviewed themes studied in the past two years. Because students are in the program for three years, it was important not to repeat any theme during that time.

At this point, students consulted the standards to see what the state said they needed to learn that they had not already considered. In Vermont, a set of standards called the Vital Results act as an umbrella for the Fields of Knowledge. The Vital Results include clusters of standards in Communication, Reasoning and Problem Solving, Personal Development, and Civic and Social Responsibility. The Fields of Knowledge support the Vital Results, and standards cluster into Arts, Language, and Literature; History and Social Sciences; and Science, Mathematics, and Technology.

The layout of Vermont's standards is particularly helpful when planning for integration because the Vital Results are broad-based and interdisciplinary in nature. Alpha students work on the Vital Results as individualized goals. Students plan to cover the Fields of Knowledge as a class. Again, the standards are relatively broad-based and do not specify particular content for mastery. History is the only area that specifies content. Interestingly, the students found the standards intriguing and challenging to work through. One student said, "Sometimes the government has good ideas."

Reading about Mark Springer and his work with student-generated questions and self-directed learning (Brown, 2002) inspired Cynthia, Meg, and Joan. They decided that it was time to involve the students in the total planning process. The selected themes this year were Infinity and Beyond; Moving into My Body: Genes to Jeans/Me, Myself, and Why?; and They Came for Peace. Students worked in three large groups in which they designed curriculum for one of the themes. Students chose the theme that they wished to work on, but the teachers also applied a selection process, if necessary, to keep the groups balanced by gender and grade level. Meg, Joan, and Cynthia each acted as a facilitator for one group. Groups explored the standards and designed the learning experiences and assessments for their theme. Then, all the students studied the three themes for the duration of the year.

Negotiating the Lesson Planning

Although the students planned all aspects of the curriculum, the planning required negotiation with the group facilitator. Negotiation meant exactly that. Both teachers and students had a voice about what they would study. The teacher also maintained the right to declare some things nonnegotiable.

In the three large groups, some very serious negotiation took place. Following is an example of the process of negotiation as it occurred for the group working on the theme They Came for Peace.

The theme involved a study of current events that occurred as the result of movements of groups of people. The teachers suggested four standards they thought could direct the planning effectively:

- **6.8. Movements and Settlements.** Students analyze the factors and implications associated with the historical and contemporary movements and settlements of people and groups in various times. (Geography)
- **4.3. Cultural Expression.** Students demonstrate understanding of the cultural expressions that are characteristic of particular groups. (Humanities and social sciences)
- **4.4. Effects of Prejudice.** Students demonstrate an understanding of the concepts of prejudice and its effects on various groups. (Humanities and social sciences)
- **5.10. Diverse Literary Traditions.** Students interpret works from diverse learning traditions. (Arts, language, and literature)

The students were not so quick to accept the teachers' judgment on the appropriate standards to guide the study. They discussed the fact that prejudice may not always be involved in a movement, and that they did not want to force standards into the curriculum where they did not belong. They also expressed concern about too much focus on culture instead of the movement; they had studied the theme Culture before. This time they wanted to focus on the causes and effects of the movement. In short, students believed that standards 4.3 and 4.4 would take away from the focus on 6.8, not add to it. The teacher found it to be an exhilarating discussion, and she fully agreed with their perspective.

The group then turned to language arts standard 5.10—Diverse Literary Traditions. Covering this standard, however, did not fit with their personal goals. They were interested in using the final theme of the year to redo work in their preferred genre if they had written good pieces all year or to correct and improve their work if they were weak in this area. Again, their logic was strong, and the teacher accepted their rationale.

In the end, students used geography standard 6.8, Movements and Settlements, to guide their planning and the Vital Results for assessment. The group used this theme to meet the personal goals they had set during their student-parent-teacher conferences.

Students completed the planning exercise by outlining the expectations they had for the thematic study. They presented this expectation sheet to their peers and their teachers for discussion. They also developed a rubric for the unit. (See Appendices C-1 and C-2 for the planning sheet and rubric, respectively.)

Assessment Practices

Alpha teachers integrate assessment into the learning experiences. Students take national standardized tests and Vermont assessments; they demonstrate repeatedly that they are learning (Smith & Myers, 2001). In addition, each student undergoes weekly peer review and teacher conferences. Although Alpha does measure student performance in traditional subject areas, students do not receive report cards with grades on subjects. Instead, Alpha uses a portfolio system that culminates with a student-parent portfolio conference three times a year.

The assessment is ongoing and involves goal setting, reflection, and self-assessment. Each student sets up his or her portfolio using Vermont's Vital Results, rather than the subject areas as the organizers (see Appendix C-3 for an example of individualized self-assessment criteria based on the Vital Results). Alpha has added a category called Functioning Independently. Thus, they divide the portfolio into the following categories:

- Communication
- Reasoning and Problem Solving
- Functioning Independently
- Personal Development
- Civic and Social Responsibility

Students are responsible for categorizing their work into each of these categories. They collect and add their work over the three years they are in the program. This allows them to compare, for example, their best work from grade 6 with their work in grade 7 or 8. The portfolio gives them an opportunity to place their work from a variety of subject areas in the same category and reinforces the connections among disciplines. It also gives the students opportunities to speak and write in the language of the state standards. A finished piece of work needs to show how it demonstrates achievement of the Vital Results standards. Where does the assignment on Origins of the Universe go and why? Where do they place the written explanation for mathematical probability? Collecting, categorizing, analyzing, and revising allow students—and their parents—to see how they learn.

The Alpha program revolves around goal setting. Students use a goals notebook to track their progress. The teachers set weekly minimum goals for all the students. Each student also chooses individualized weekly goals from the Vermont Vital Results. The students record these goals as assignments on the left-hand side of their goals notebooks. All students write well-developed self-assessments and hand them in to the teachers every Thursday.

At the beginning of each year, the younger students pair up with senior students as "goals partners." The older student acts as a mentor for the younger student. The program works on a three-year cycle, so the younger students become mentors later. Each week, students discuss their work with their goals partners and their teachers, who help them after school if there's a problem.

Students receive written guidelines for evaluation, or they create their own assessments. Sixth grade students, or new students in the program, pair up with older students who walk them through an orientation to the program. The veteran student also performs mock peer assessments. In addition, they lead the newer students through a mock student-led parent conference, complete with work samples, probing questions, and written feedback.

Grade 6 students concentrate on organizing their portfolios around the Vital Results. By 7th grade, students can sort their work with some support. By 8th grade, students sort their work independently and are eager to discuss with parents what they have accomplished.

A student-parent-teacher conference is held once each trimester. Both students and parents speak very positively about this experience. Parents have the opportunity to read and assess their child's portfolio each trimester. When they attend this one- to three-hour portfolio conference led by their child, the teacher moves in and out of this meeting. At the conference, students show evidence that they have achieved their goals and have demonstrated the standards.

A result of the conference is that students, teachers, and parents are involved in establishing the next set of goals. As the trimester progresses, the weekly goals appear on a progress sheet listing successes and continued challenges. This process also helps students to set new goals for the next semester.

Academic Success

In 2003, the Alpha program was one of two in the United States to win the National Middle School Association's "Teams That Make a Difference" award for academic excellence. This significant success is an excellent indicator that bridging accountability and relevance is possible. This is particularly significant considering that the Alpha program does not concern itself specifically with preparing for state tests or with carefully delineating different discipline expectations for different grades. (The exception is math, which is taught separately to the different grades.)

Carol Smith, an educational consultant who recently retired from Alpha after 25 years, was instrumental in shaping the team's philosophy and its success. She continues her involvement, in part, by analyzing quantitative data on test scores. The New Standards English Language Arts Reference Exam (NSRE) and the New Standards Mathematical Reference Exam are mandated, standards-based state tests prepared by Harcourt-Brace. Results from 1998 to 2000 indicate that Alpha students consistently produced results at or above those of the rest of the school, the district, and the state on both the math and literature tests. Students also did well on nationally standardized tests. In 2000, for example, Alpha 7th graders did as well as, or better than, their counterparts on the Stanford Achievement Test in 13 areas, including reading, math, and thinking skills. Only in spelling did they rank slightly below others.

Cynthia, Joan, and Meg postulate that student success on standards-based tests is related to the fact that the NSRE test actually adopts Alpha's methods of teaching and learning. Students are accustomed to exploring their learning in depth rather than simply learning facts. Thus, it is a natural process to answer a typical question on an NSRE exam. Such a question might ask students to read and analyze a passage, support the analysis by referring to the text, and connect it to personal experience.

Does Alpha Work?

Many intriguing practices that are part of the Alpha program can help us fully understand the experience. For example, students call teachers by their first names to indicate that close relationships are welcome. Issues brought up in classroom meetings must end in consensus and never in a vote. In practice, this means that although students may not agree with each decision, they must feel that they have a voice in the decision. Everyone participates in whole-group projects, such as the camping trip at the end of the year. Each year, students make a quilt and sell it in a raffle to raise money so that the entire team can go on the trip. All students work on the quilt in some way. The camping trip is a way to develop team-building skills as well as say good-bye to the 8th grade students and welcome the 6th and 7th graders as next year's new team leaders.

Here are some of the students' comments about Alpha:

> This is the best program for me.
>
> Alpha was my third choice, and I was surprised when they told me I was in the program. Now I really like it. (A student in his sixth week of the program)
>
> It's a great program. It's not just about work; it's about preparing for life. It's a great base for high school. You learn to organize and communicate and have good relationships with kids in grade 6, 7, and 8, as well as with the teachers.

Here is what some of the parents said:

> High-school teachers can identify Alpha students because they approach learning differently—they know how to ask questions.
>
> It's a great program. My son would have succeeded in any program, but because he went to Alpha, he looks at his work and analyzes his successes and weaknesses. He asks, "How do I get from here to where I want to go?"
>
> These kids learn to go way beyond normal expectations because a grade is not important. It's really good for learning life skills, too.

Does Alpha work for the teachers? For Cynthia, Joan, and Meg, the answer is an unqualified yes. Such a program could not exist without the dedication of exemplary teachers who are willing to put their philosophies into action. Yet it is probably true that not every teacher would fit into Alpha. Similarly, the parents, teachers, and students are quick to acknowledge that Alpha does not suit every parent. In addition, perhaps not every student is suited for Alpha, although this was an unanswered question in our discussions.

We believe that all educators can learn many lessons from Alpha. The most obvious factor for success is students' responsibility for their own learning—from deciding on the content based on standards and student interests, to creating interesting learning activities, to taking charge, in part, of their own assessment. The support of both teachers and parents is critical for student success. These ingredients seem to be integral to the success of this innovative and long-standing program that demonstrates that curriculum can be both relevant and rigorous.

11 Questions and Answers

Integrating the curriculum is a challenging undertaking, and because most teachers have little experience with it, they typically have many questions. This chapter answers some of the questions we encounter most frequently.

What happens when subjects do not fit together?

The scan-and-cluster process described in detail in Chapter 4 helps teachers find natural fits or potential areas for integration. Teachers should include only those concepts and skills that fit together naturally and validly in an integrated unit. They should never force integration or choose activities that are superficial and do not address important concepts and skills within disciplines.

Sometimes after teaching a unit and reflecting on its effectiveness, teachers discover additional disciplinary concepts and skills that they can integrate. This was true with the Medieval Times unit described in Chapter 7. Although mathematics was not included originally, upon reflection, teachers discovered several opportunities to integrate mathematics the next time they taught the unit. Often, bringing in the expert in the subject area that does not fit helps the team discover all sorts of ways to include that subject legitimately.

How do I keep a record of the standards I have covered?

The easiest way to keep a record of the standards covered is to use an electronic curriculum planner that contains the standards or a hyperlink to them. For example, Curriculum Creator, a Web-based curriculum planner developed at the Appalachia Educational Laboratory (http://www.ael.org /curriculumcreator), allows teachers to link learning activities to standards. Curriculum Creator also provides cumulative reports that show which standards the teachers have covered and how many times they taught each standard.

If an electronic planner is not available, use a paper form that lists all standards. Then, record the standards as you design and teach the integrated units. Some school districts provide a scope and sequence of instruction that indicates which standards to teach during each grading period. In any case, we recommend that teachers think of meaningful chunks of standards when they select them for a unit.

How do I deal with standardized tests?

We believe that not everything important is tested, and not everything tested is necessarily important. For example, standardized tests do not measure skills in oral language, yet we know the importance of effective oral communication and its impact on students' ability to develop good written communication skills. Also, the BE component of the KNOW/DO/BE cannot be tested by standardized measures. However, it is an extremely important part of a child's education. Therefore, educators need to exercise judgment about what is most important for students to KNOW and be able to DO, and how they should BE, as they are designing curriculum.

Developing standards-based units following the processes described in this book can help us "deal with the test" as well. If the test is not criterion-referenced, teachers need to compare the standards with the test objectives to determine what important concepts and skills they need to cover.

Reviewing standardized test results is an important part of curriculum planning. We need to identify which concepts and skills students have mastered and which ones need special attention before designing curriculum. In the era of the No Child Left Behind Act and other accountability measures, teachers need to determine the learning needs of specific groups of students, such as different minority groups, as well as the needs of individual students. This means differentiating instruction within a unit so that all students are learning the same concepts and skills but are not necessarily doing the same thing at the same time. Using learning centers, building curriculum around student questions, and allowing students to design individual projects can help meet the needs of all learners.

If the BE is so important, how do we measure it?

The BE may never be measured in the same way as, for example, math and science skills. Yet, as Tony Giblin of Brock University in Ontario reminds us, teachers are modeling life skills, or the BE, all of the time. According to Tony, students need to learn ways to BE in the world. They do not necessarily know how to behave in acceptable ways. Or they may be aware that they do not have social skills but may not know exactly what those skills are. The teacher can introduce the skills and allow time for practice until students internalize them.

At River School, a charter school in Napa, California, teachers work hard to develop an entire school culture that teaches character through both the explicit and the "implicit curriculum" (Inlay, 2003). Although teachers rarely discuss character, they promote it in the school culture at every opportunity. They concentrate on fostering personal responsibility and social responsibility through modeling and directing student awareness to these characteristics during the daily school events. Teachers listen to students and take their concerns seriously. They have homeroom advisories and listening groups. Students help to develop the curriculum and hold teacher-

parent-student conferences for assessment purposes. Teachers measure the success of the implicit curriculum when students

- Are active rather than passive (actors not victims),
- Feel it is safe to make a mistake,
- Treat others fairly on the playground, and
- Express opinions backed by logic.

How do I find the time for integrated curriculum?

Designing standards-based integrated curriculum ultimately saves time. Many who have designed integrated curriculum say it is the only way to cover all of the standards. When we integrate curriculum, we are working smarter, not harder. However, when teachers first use the backward design process to develop a unit, they will need more time than was previously necessary. This is because most are not accustomed to thinking in this way when they plan curriculum. Schools and school districts should offer time in the summer, or on noninstructional days, for the initial curriculum work. Some schools provide team planning time, which offers an opportunity for those who teach the same grade to work together on curriculum mapping and unit design. After their first experience with the process, teachers will find that designing standards-based, integrated units becomes easier and is less time-consuming.

Auburn High School in Riner, Virginia, is one of many schools that create extra time for curriculum work and teacher collaboration. At Auburn, if an interdisciplinary team did not have common planning time, the principal scheduled them to have the same lunchtime, followed by a duty period. The principal released these teachers from hall duty so they had extended planning time. At Newsome Park Elementary, featured in Chapter 9, students come early four days each week and leave at 12:30 on Wednesday. This provides the teachers with extra planning time on Wednesday afternoons, while maintaining the integrity of instructional time. Many schools have devised similar ways to use extended instructional days to allow time for planning one day each week or every other week. Some school districts use professional development days and teacher workdays for curriculum work as well. Schools that adopt a year-round calendar have three-week intersessions between quarters. The intersessions permit concentrated time for teachers to collaborate on curriculum design. Teachers receive either compensatory time or stipends for this work. Finally, some school districts have lengthened the traditional school year to allow more time for curriculum work.

What is the role of administrators?

In our experience, administrators play a key role in supporting the use of integrated curriculum. They act as supporters, facilitators, barrier removers, and resource finders. Here are some examples of the supports they can offer:

- Scheduling common planning time
- Creating flexible space
- Providing autonomy for teams to create their own curriculum, schedules, and systems for monitoring student progress
- Sponsoring professional development

When Rebecca worked with four Virginia secondary schools on developing interdisciplinary, teamed instruction, teachers in the project identified the facilitative role of administrators as (1) participating in the team process and (2) expressing support for interdisciplinary curriculum to others (Burns, 1995). Other principals have identified their role in curriculum integration similarly, as resource provider, visionary, coordinator, support system for teachers, and asker of "what if" questions to help teachers think through their curriculum plans (Brazee & Capelluti, 1994).

Administrators also should meet with interdisciplinary teams regularly to provide them with student performance data from standardized tests, mandated curriculum requirements, instructional resources that align with standards, and other important information that may come from the state or the district. Administrators can review teachers' curriculum maps and lesson plans, observe their classes, and provide constructive feedback on how well they are aligning curriculum, instruction, and assessment with standards.

When administrators are truly committed to integrated curriculum, teachers are far more likely to invest the time and effort required to plan and implement it successfully.

What kind of space do we need to implement integrated curriculum?

Most integrated programs make do with traditional spaces. Susan worked at Merritton High School, District School Board of Niagara, Ontario, on a variety of integrated projects. No large classrooms were available, but teachers sometimes combined as many as three classes for special events. They used their ingenuity to create new spaces. The gym became an instructional space when physical education students were outside, an old boiler room sufficed for larger meetings, the cafeteria housed large-group meetings, and many small-group meetings actually took place in the hall.

Many integrated programs do have the luxury of working in alternative spaces. Some schools use a school-within-a-school approach in which teachers on a particular team, or at a particular grade level, have their instructional space in close proximity on one floor or in one wing of the building. Four teachers may each have a small classroom. Students rotate back and forth

between classrooms. Classes also may meet in a large group if there are folding doors between two classrooms, or if a large-group meeting space is available.

Some school planners design facilities with integrated curriculum in mind. A team of teachers, administrators, and architects designed Capital High School in Charleston, West Virginia, to accommodate several three-member humanities teams (English, social studies, and fine arts). Three large humanities centers (one for each grade) included "wet areas" for hands-on artwork, individual study carrels, tables for small-group work, computers, a classroom-style area, a mini-library, display space for student work, and private teacher-student conference space. Teachers shared several classrooms for instruction and used workrooms for team planning (Burns, 1995).

How do I enlist parental support?

Effective and frequent communication is the key to enlisting parental support. Newsletters are one tool for regular communication with parents. At Stonewall Jackson Middle School in Charleston, West Virginia, the principal sends a newsletter to parents monthly. Every edition includes information about what each of the interdisciplinary teams is planning, such as integrated curriculum units, special programs, upcoming projects or assignments, and field trips. The teams also acknowledge student accomplishments, such as who made the honor roll or who had the best attendance. When parents know about curriculum plans, they can support their children's learning at home. Parents also are pleased to see their children's accomplishments recognized in print.

Stonewall Jackson Middle School, like many schools, uses student-led parent conferences. Parents are more likely to attend conferences when their students are involved, and parents have the opportunity to see firsthand that their children are learning. Many of these schools also use interdisciplinary team conferences, during which parents meet with all teachers on the team together. This gives parents a better perspective on team expectations, goals, activities, and challenges. They also have an opportunity to ask questions and to offer resources they may be able to contribute to the team's efforts.

Some teachers or interdisciplinary teams believe they should contact parents regularly with good news about their children. Once every grading period, teachers may call parents to say something positive about their child's progress. In other schools, teachers send portfolios or individual assignments home for parental signatures and responses. Many primary schools are using *Family Connections,* a newsletter and guide for parents developed at Appalachia Educational Laboratory (http://www.ael.org). *Family Connections* consists of 30 issues, each with activities for parents to do with their children at home that support learning across

the curriculum. Teachers also may personalize the newsletter with a special message about each child.

How do I schedule classes to make interdisciplinary curriculum work?

If integrated curriculum is a school's desired approach, then scheduling should be a top priority. Teams need time to plan together. They also should share the same students. Furthermore, they need flexibility to use longer blocks of time for learning experiences. For example, in a middle school, an interdisciplinary team of four may have a 200-minute block of time. Teachers may choose to use that block in different ways for different purposes. One day they may want to bring in a special program or speaker, or take a field trip, and use all or most of the block for the large-group activity. Another day, the English teacher may have students working on a special writing assignment that requires extra time to complete. On that day, the team might decide to allow 90 minutes for the English assignment and divide the remaining time between the other classes, or even to eliminate some classes on that day. On other days, a different teacher may need extra time. Sometimes the team may decide to divide the time evenly among the four classes.

In many elementary schools, teachers use a daily or weekly scheduling format to decide how they can structure time for integrated activities. For example, Newsome Park Elementary School in Newport News, Virginia (see Chapter 9), structures the weekly and daily instructional time to provide a focus on project-based learning. Teachers must also allow time for short units on concepts and skills that they do not cover in the project. Sometimes, they need to use direct instruction on specific skills.

More and more high schools are using organizational strategies such as school-within-a-school, freshman transition, small learning communities, or career academies. In these programs, several teachers work with the same group of students during a block of time or at different times throughout the day or week, depending on the type of block schedule they use. Each of these programs has a specific focus. A health sciences academy, for example, might include biology, English, social studies, mathematics, and health career studies. A freshman transition program can use an interdisciplinary approach similar to what the students experienced in middle school. A small learning community devoted to the study of arts and humanities might include art, music, literature and writing, and history. Some high schools schedule back-to-back blocks of complementary subjects such as math and science, or English and social studies, to support integration.

How many years do I need to teach before I can integrate the curriculum?

You can do it the very first year! Marie Ciafre, a dynamic teacher at Newsome Park Elementary School (see Chapter 9), is a first-year teacher. She searched the Internet to find a school that was using an integrated approach and now teaches at Newsome Park Elementary in the project-based approach. Adrian DeTullio (see Chapters 6 and 7) and Sonja Upton, Ellie Phillips, and Melissa Rubocki (see Chapters 4 and 5) are all in their early years of teaching. At the same time, many veteran teachers are beginning the journey toward curriculum integration. This work is energizing them. Experience is not a prerequisite for designing integrated curriculum. Using the template in Chapter 6, or other designs described in this book, any teacher can create integrated curriculum with some perseverance and a little positive risk taking!

What do we do with the textbooks?

Textbooks are only one resource. Other instructional resources are available, such as the Internet and the community itself. Teachers should not be dependent on textbooks, but rather should consider them as only one of many instructional resources.

In addition, textbooks are changing what they present to students and how they present it. The publishers are making efforts to align their material with standards. However, given the varying levels of complexity in different states' standards, this is an almost impossible task. Although publishers claim that textbooks are aligned with state standards and testing, in reality most publishers write their material for the states that have the largest market.

The upside of the textbook debate is that most publishers are providing interdisciplinary connections in the materials they present. Most include ancillary interdisciplinary materials, such as music, artwork, and other related material on CDs that a school or district may purchase. These materials can aid the integration process.

The bottom line is that the textbooks are not the curriculum. We recommend that teachers design their curriculum and then scan the textbooks to identify the concepts and important ideas they can use to support the curriculum. Other instructional materials, such as field trips, projects, writing assignments, library research, the Internet, community resources, and hands-on activities can support student learning.

We have access to an electronic planner. It tells what standards we have covered and saves us time. Can't we use that to integrate the curriculum?

Using an electronic planner can help connect learning activities and assessments to standards. However, the electronic planners on the market today do not provide a template for designing integrated curriculum. In fact, using an electronic planner without doing preliminary planning might actually sabotage integrated curriculum design. Many of them are discipline-based and do not make connections across the disciplines. Teachers are still the curriculum architects and must do the initial planning. We recommend that they begin by using a template such as the one in Chapter 6. Once the planning process is complete, the electronic planner can help align the curricular focus and the teaching and assessment strategies to the standards. The planner also provides an archive of what standards teachers have covered, but it cannot do the planning for them.

I don't know enough about other subjects, especially music. How do I teach them?

This is a very natural and common fear, and there are several approaches to overcoming it. First, the teacher needs to be comfortable saying to students, "I don't know the answer to that question. Let's find it out together." Willingness to learn about other subjects can lead to interesting discoveries that teachers can incorporate into an integrated curriculum. Sometimes students may have knowledge or skill in music or another subject that they can contribute to the class's learning. Perhaps one of the parents, another teacher, or a friend in the community can come into the classroom and provide instruction on a particular subject.

Middle and high schools have specialists in music and art on staff. It makes sense to include them on an interdisciplinary team. Some elementary schools have specialists as well; however, smaller schools may share them with one or more schools. This requires advance planning with the specialists so they can be present to carry out their part of the integrated unit.

Should we start small or try to do something big on our first try?

Many educators say, "We are thinking big about integrated curriculum, but starting small." As teachers gain experience with the planning process, they become more comfortable with it. Successful implementation of a short integrated unit can lead to broadened plans for the next time. In fact, planning too much the first time around is a sure route to failure. A short unit may last only two weeks. The next time around, teachers may plan a four- to six-week unit. A series of these units can add up to a full year's integrated program.

What happens if I don't use the KNOW/DO/BE framework?

The important thing is to use some kind of framework. In this book, we describe three

successful integrated programs that use a framework other than KNOW/DO/BE (see Chapters 8, 9, and 10). However, all of these programs use some process for identifying the KNOW, DO, and BE. They are all standards-based with instruction and assessment aligned. As well, they include content, learning activities, and assessments that are relevant and engaging for students.

I have so many resources that I can just look up, and then I will have a sound integrated curriculum. Why should I reinvent the wheel?

A sound integrated curriculum is coherent. Looking up resources and putting them together does not necessarily lead to a coherent, or significant, study. It is an easy tack to take, because there are some very good ideas available. Without proper planning for both accountability and relevance, however, the curriculum is nothing more than a series of activities. Students may miss the "So what?" of learning. Teachers must think like assessors as well as activity designers through every step of the curriculum planning process. They also need to include students' questions and concerns in the planning. Putting together resources without first designing the integrated unit eliminates the student voice. It also omits the vital components of relevance and alignment with standards.

It is so hard to find enduring understandings. Yet they seem so simple when you do find them. Why bother?

Enduring understandings are the heart of teaching. They are the most important things for students to learn. Paradoxically, they are simple and profound at the same time. To work at higher levels of thinking, we need to identify the enduring understandings and spend a lot of time studying them.

Some states offer documents that facilitate work in this realm. Teachers should check with their district office or state department of education to see what material is available to assist them with curriculum planning. Some states have done the work of identifying essential learnings. For example, the Virginia Department of Education (http://www.pen.k12.va.us) provides teachers with a Resource Guide that identifies essential learnings (enduring understandings) for each standard. The Michigan Department of Education's Web site (http://www.michigan.gov/mde) contains an abundance of helpful information for teachers. The department has identified key concepts and skills for all the standards. They go further by suggesting particular topics for units, with instructional resources, assessments, and performance expectations.

Who should be on an interdisciplinary planning team? How many people should there be?

Teachers who are committed to interdisciplinary approaches should be on a planning team. They should also be the people who will teach the curriculum. Usually an effective team is composed of individuals with complementary rather than similar talents and teaching styles. Diversity gives the team an edge in meeting the needs of all students. However, team members should have three characteristics in common: energy, persistence, and commitment to change (Burns, 1995).

The number of teachers on a team varies considerably from school to school. Frequently, a team has four teachers representing English, science, math, and social studies. However, some schools use two-person teams with each teacher being responsible for instruction in two content areas. Some schools use three-person teams. For example, each team has an English teacher, a science teacher, and a math teacher. Each team member also teaches social studies. Frequently, special educators work with the core teams, and specialist teachers rotate among the teams. Some high schools use an academy model that may include as many as five teachers—four from the academic disciplines and one from a vocational or career cluster area. More than seven on a team is too many.

Elementary teachers work a little differently. At the primary grades, they tend to use self-contained classrooms, but the grade-level teachers plan instruction together so there is consistency across all classrooms. At upper-elementary grades, teachers frequently specialize in one or more subjects, and students rotate between them during the day or several times each week. Some elementary teachers rotate their students for different units depending on the interests of the teachers or the students.

What do we do when one person takes control or sabotages the planning process?

Teams sometimes experience conflict. Susan knows this from personal experience, having been involved in a number of curriculum design teams. Teams should remember that team interactions follow a pattern, and there are four stages in team building: forming, storming, norming, and performing (Tuckman, as cited in Maurer, 1994). The team forms together, and, after working together for a while, they develop group norms. Only then can they perform.

The conflict happens before norms are established. Teams may find they need to work through a conflict resolution process.

On occasion, the conflict cannot be resolved. At this point, it is better to reconfigure the team. Not everyone is naturally a team player. Some teachers do much better on their own than on a team.

As a team member or a team leader, Susan found she was always trying to bring the dissenters on board. This was particularly true in a large-school context where she worked on a small team and was trying to convince the rest of the school of the worth of their project. Her colleagues reminded her constantly, "Don't water the rocks." It was a hard, but valuable, lesson to learn. She was beating her head against the wall with the nonbelievers. However, when she used her energy working with other teachers who did believe in interdisciplinary approaches, good things happened. The response of students to integrated approaches went a long way in changing the minds of the rest of the school. The moral of the story: collaborate with like-minded folks. Water the seedlings and the flowers.

12

The Future of Integrated Curriculum
Stilling the Pendulum

In this book we present compelling reasons to integrate the curriculum. Yet interdisciplinary approaches are not always the order of the day. Historically in education, the pendulum has swung from one side to the other—from a traditional, disciplined-based approach to a more interdisciplinary one that was presumably more relevant. Experienced educators often remark, "What goes around comes around." In fact, we often heard this comment from teachers trying to avoid getting involved when interdisciplinary approaches were popular in the early 1990s. At that time, some teachers sat back and waited for "it" to go away. Indeed, they were right. Integrated curriculum did go away. In its place, the pendulum swung quite violently from exploring interdisciplinary approaches that increase relevancy for students to staying strictly within the boundaries of the disciplines to establish accountability. Ironically, this shift was usually even less popular with these teachers than integrated curriculum!

Will the pendulum swing again? When will educators recognize that standards and standardization alone do not work miracles? Will we move toward integration in another short-lived effort to regain relevance in our classrooms? Will we be forever dealing with a pendulum that swings from one side to another?

We think not. Rather, we believe the pendulum is stilling. The shifting back and forth between the two polarities is necessary as educators find new ways to be both accountable and to create relevant curriculum. However, the distance in the arc of the pendulum is becoming smaller and smaller. It reminds us of our initial conflicts that we discussed in Chapter 4 (see Figure 4.1). We realized that the choice was not either/or between accountability and relevance. Rather the most effective choice was both/and.

Evidence of Sustainability

Quantitative, as well as qualitative, data now support the use of integrated curriculum. We have cited numerous studies whose results indicate that students in integrated settings frequently outperform their counterparts in discipline-based settings. Additionally, the schools described in this book, all of which have used interdisciplinary approaches for several years, conducted their own research on student achievement. Their standardized test data show significant increases in student achievement and in some cases a narrowing of the achievement gap between minority and majority students. Additional data from these schools show decreases in absenteeism and discipline referrals and increases in attendance. Moreover, teachers tell us that using an integrated approach has renewed

them professionally and helped them engage students in learning. Why would we want to design only discipline-based curriculum when external and school-based studies point to the success of integration in improving teaching and learning?

The future of integrated curriculum is further supported by professional organizations such as the National Council of Teachers of English (http://www.ncte.org), the National Council of Teachers of Mathematics (http://www.nctm.org), the National Middle School Association (http://www.nmsa.org), and the National Science Foundation (http://www.nsf.org). Their Web sites, publications, and recommended curricula advance the case for integration within and beyond the disciplines. Some states and provinces now provide recommendations, lessons, and resources that assist teachers in developing interdisciplinary approaches to standards. See, for example, the Ontario Interdisciplinary Studies program (http://www.edu.gov.on.ca) and the Michigan Department of Education's curriculum guides for K–12 educators (http://www.michigan.gov/mde).

From our perspective, the world of education is fundamentally changing. In April 2003, Susan attended a session at the Learning Through the Arts (LTTA) International Conference in Ontario. Under artist educator Linda Hankin, she joined a group of teachers to create puppets out of natural materials and then participate in a play about a tree. Then she danced with

Tracey Houser to learn about potential and kinetic energy. Finally, she learned a number of math skills through constructing puppets with Matthew Romain.

Susan found all her conference sessions were fun, informative, and exciting—and these were only 3 of 40 choices. All the presenters were artist educators who coplan with teachers in schools. Their teacher partners were equally enthusiastic. Each presentation included a handout that identified the standards covered, described teaching strategies, and offered the rubrics used to measure student learning. Interestingly, the LTTA program has substantive quantitative evidence to demonstrate improved student achievement, better attitudes, and better classroom behavior (http://www.ltta.ca).

In the same week, Susan attended another conference where she met with science educators from Spain, England, the Netherlands, Germany, and Canada. Participants discussed current efforts to create an integrated science program in each country. The conversation also explored how to connect science to other disciplines. The educators particularly felt the need to make science relevant to students and to connect to the real world.

The conversations at these conferences were significantly different than they would have been a decade ago. Everyone was interested in both accountability and relevance. Education in classrooms is different, too, although teachers may not recognize this. Educators everywhere now think in terms of standards and assessment, even if they vocally oppose accountability measures. And many are actively seeking ways to make the curriculum more relevant at the same time they express concern about accountability.

In Rebecca's work with state departments of education, school districts, and schools, she has observed a significant change in educators' attitudes toward integrated curriculum. Most now ask for help in integrating curriculum around standards, whereas five years ago they said, "We can't think about integration because we have too many standards to cover in each discipline." Now these same educators are saying, "Integration is the only way we can cover all the standards." For example, Rebecca worked with the West Virginia Department of Education to assist K–4 teachers in designing standards-based, integrated units. Administrators and teachers both agreed that there was no other way to make sense of the vast number of standards primary students must master.

Middle schools and high schools are recognizing that adding on additional courses, as they did in the 1980s and 1990s, is not a sensible or realistic way to meet new requirements. There are not enough hours in the day or staff available to teach all the new requirements, or to address the increasing knowledge explosion in all the disciplines. Educators are beginning to realize that they can integrate requirements such as character education into each course or integrated unit by using the KNOW/DO/BE process. The BE represents the components of character education that students should learn. Furthermore, they acknowledge that teaching students interdisciplinary concepts and skills prepares them for acquiring and using new knowledge as it becomes available. These interdisciplinary concepts and skills mirror the requirements for success in the world of work and real-life problem solving and decision making.

In May 2003, Rebecca visited Southeast Raleigh High School in Raleigh, North Carolina. Southeast is a recipient of a Smaller Learning Communities grant from the U.S. Department of Education's Office of Vocational and Adult Education. During the three years of the grant, Southeast has designed a program called Career-Focused Learning Communities (CFLC). These communities include integrated academic and career-focused courses. Two communities are in place—one in medicine/biotechnology and another in information technology. Communities for digital arts and engineering are scheduled to be added in fall 2003. Within each CFLC, a team of teachers integrates studies in the career field. They also work with core academic teachers and others to make interdisciplinary connections across the curriculum that closely align with the North Carolina standards and required courses of study. Students also apply their learning during job shadowing and apprenticeships at local businesses, hospitals, or colleges and universities. Furthermore, students experience active learning in their classes and produce products and presentations on a regular basis. In their senior year, all students complete an interdisciplinary project and present it to a panel of two teachers and a community member for evaluation.

According to Southeast administrators and teachers, the integrated programs have been successful in changing the culture of the school to reflect greater emphasis on academics, improved student-teacher relationships, and enhanced opportunities for relevance through learning in the community. Furthermore, standardized test scores continue to rise, and the achievement gap between African American and white students has decreased significantly. Eighty percent of Southeast students now pass their end-of-course exams required by the state. However, the principal, John Modest, says, "We can still do better!"

Our Vision of the Future of Education

Reflecting on our experience with integrated curriculum over the past decade, we predict that in the 21st century the pendulum will not swing as violently from accountability to relevance. Instead, modified accountability measures will replace the more stringent and sometimes meaningless standardized measures. The modified measures will include assessments that double as learning strategies and provide space for interdisciplinary approaches. Accountability, in this more palatable form, will remain at the center of successful educational practice.

Yet, accountability is not enough. The curriculum must also be relevant. A meaningful curriculum that motivates student learning is also at the center of successful practice. Both accountability and relevance are the focus of effective teaching.

As the educators featured in this book demonstrate, integrated curriculum has the potential to satisfy both prerogatives. It can be both accountable and relevant. Thus, we believe the stage is set for the reemergence of integrated curriculum in a form that is here to stay. Interdisciplinary approaches have the potential to help quiet the pendulum. This is a welcome relief and one that allows teachers the time to explore how to integrate the curriculum in ways that are most effective for students.

Educators, as a collective, are beginning to make sense of and put into practice a BOTH/AND vision of education. Integrated curriculum is at the core of this vision. Figure 12.1 illustrates our representation of a BOTH/AND view of education.

In this context, the pendulum stills. A gentle swaying continues as educators learn

12.1 A BOTH/AND Vision of Education

BOTH	AND
Accountability	Relevance
KNOW/DO	BE
Disciplinary concepts and skills	Set in the context of a wider umbrella of interdisciplinary skills and concepts
Specialization in later years	Set in the context of the wider real world
Identification of criteria for interdisciplinary skills and direct instruction for them	Applied across subject areas
Standardized or written tests	Performance-based assessment
Quantitative measures	Qualitative measures
Teachers collaboratively planning with other teachers	Students collaboratively planning with teachers
Teacher-generated questions	Student-generated questions
Traditional instructional strategies (e.g., lecture, phonics)	Set in a more holistic context (e.g., lecture set in the context of active learning and a variety of instructional strategies; phonics set in the context of whole language)

more about how to make the learning experience more effective. This time, instead of "what goes around comes around," it's "what goes around and is effective for student learning stays around."

We believe that the time is both right and ripe for reintroducing integrated approaches. Integrated curriculum—done thoughtfully—can address both accountability and relevance needs. The examples in this book prove it. This does not mean that integration has to be all day, every day. We expect that the immediate future will look much like the past; there will be pockets of integrated projects across our schools. However, we predict that slowly and surely interdisciplinary approaches will expand to

become a norm rather than an anomaly. Such approaches, in turn, will receive increasing support from policy documents such as those that now exist in places such as Ontario, Quebéc, and Taiwan.

Committed teachers now understand that the only way to cover the standards and provide constructive assessment is to integrate. They are lighting the path for others as teachers become increasingly comfortable with standards and come to this realization.

We invite you to help light this path. It is a reenergizing and exciting place to be. Education will never be the same again. Welcome to the adventure.

Appendix A

Interdisciplinary Curriculum Template for the Medieval Times Unit

1. Scan and cluster standards vertically and horizontally to select one or two broad-based standards for each discipline in the integrated unit.

- Design and make a pulley and gear system and investigate how motion is transferred from one system to another. (Science)
- Formulate questions about and identify needs and problems related to structures and mechanisms in their environment and explore possible solutions and answers. (Science)
- Produce two- and three-dimensional works of art that communicate ideas for specific purposes and to specific audiences. (The arts)
- Begin to develop research skills. (Social studies, science)
- Identify the distinguishing features of a medieval society. (Social studies)
- Communicate ideas and information for a variety of purposes and to specific audiences. (Language)
- Contribute and work constructively in groups. (Language)

2. Choose an age-appropriate and relevant topic/theme.

> **Medieval Times**

3. Create a web to identify potential clusters of standards/content.

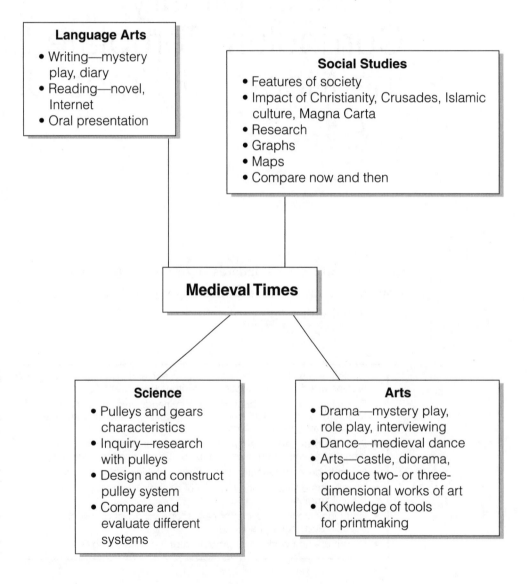

Language Arts

- Writing—mystery play, diary
- Reading—novel, Internet
- Oral presentation

Social Studies

- Features of society
- Impact of Christianity, Crusades, Islamic culture, Magna Carta
- Research
- Graphs
- Maps
- Compare now and then

Medieval Times

Science

- Pulleys and gears characteristics
- Inquiry—research with pulleys
- Design and construct pulley system
- Compare and evaluate different systems

Arts

- Drama—mystery play, role play, interviewing
- Dance—medieval dance
- Arts—castle, diorama, produce two- or three-dimensional works of art
- Knowledge of tools for printmaking

4. Construct a KNOW/DO/BE bridge.

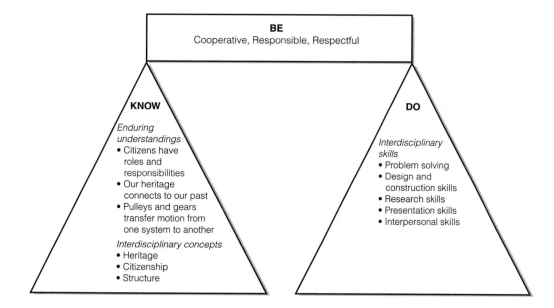

5. Design a culminating assessment.

You are a citizen of St. Ann's village. It is time for the Medieval Festival. Many visitors are coming to your festival. Some will come from as far away as the 21st century. They will be curious about how you live, the culture, and how it has affected their culture today. You are to research one aspect of medieval times and how it is represented today. You have three responsibilities:

1. You and a partner are in charge of a booth at the fair. Small groups will visit you. You are responsible for

   - An oral presentation of your independent research. (Oral presentation)
   - A storyboard outlining the important facts about your research. (Written presentation)
   - An activity that your visitors can do that will teach them something about your area of research. For example, you might make a working catapult or design a game. (Design and construction)
   - Answering questions that the visitors have and comparing what you have discovered from medieval times with the culture in the 21st century. (Research)

2. You are responsible for contributing to the archives. Please select from the artifacts you have created during the unit: castle with blueprints, stained glass windows, maps. Provide a written report of how your artifact is represented in the 21st century. (Design and construction)

3. It was very common to have mystery plays performed during medieval times. Your group is to write and perform a mystery play for the audience during the festival. (Oral presentation)

There will be teacher, self-, and peer assessment.

6. Create guiding questions.

- Why are people today still interested in medieval times?
- How did people live in medieval times?
- How do pulleys and gears work, and how did the people use them in medieval times?
- How do the important events of medieval times affect our culture today?

7. Generate instructional activities and assessments aligned with the KNOW/DO/BE bridge and the culminating assessment:

(a) Recluster standards to develop mini-units.

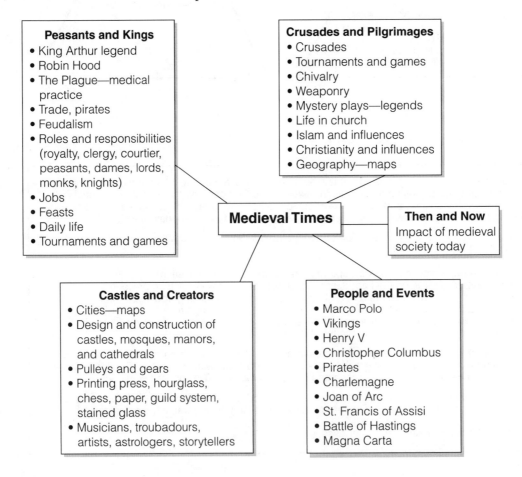

Peasants and Kings
- King Arthur legend
- Robin Hood
- The Plague—medical practice
- Trade, pirates
- Feudalism
- Roles and responsibilities (royalty, clergy, courtier, peasants, dames, lords, monks, knights)
- Jobs
- Feasts
- Daily life
- Tournaments and games

Crusades and Pilgrimages
- Crusades
- Tournaments and games
- Chivalry
- Weaponry
- Mystery plays—legends
- Life in church
- Islam and influences
- Christianity and influences
- Geography—maps

Medieval Times

Then and Now
Impact of medieval society today

Castles and Creators
- Cities—maps
- Design and construction of castles, mosques, manors, and cathedrals
- Pulleys and gears
- Printing press, hourglass, chess, paper, guild system, stained glass
- Musicians, troubadours, artists, astrologers, storytellers

People and Events
- Marco Polo
- Vikings
- Henry V
- Christopher Columbus
- Pirates
- Charlemagne
- Joan of Arc
- St. Francis of Assisi
- Battle of Hastings
- Magna Carta

(b) Create standards-based learning experiences with built-in assessment.

Mini-Unit: Kings and Peasants

Teaching/learning experiences	Standards	Assessment
In groups, students brainstorm for typical questions a researcher would ask to discover how people lived in the Middle Ages. Class develops generic questions. They should include categories such as food, clothes, homes, entertainment, work, government, trade, transportation, conflict mediation.	• Identify the distinguishing features of medieval society. (SS) • Use appropriate vocabulary to describe their inquiries and observations. (SS)	The questions that the class generates will be written on newsprint and displayed for the class and the teacher to evaluate for completeness.
In triads, students do an in-depth research study to provide answers to research questions for one group in medieval society. Groups include peasants, royalty, knights, clergy, lords and ladies, townspeople, explorers, traders.	• Ask pertinent questions to gain information. (SS) • Locate relevant information from a variety of sources. (SS) • Analyze, clarify, and interpret information about the social, political, and economic structures of medieval society. (SS) • Begin to develop research skills. (L) • Construct and read a chart. (SS) • Use appropriate strategies to organize and carry out a group project. (L)	• Charts with the student-generated questions will be given to triads. Students will fill in with information they generated from the research done. • Teacher and self-evaluation.
Students create a diorama from a shoebox that illustrates a typical scene from their assigned social group.	• Produce two- and three-dimensional works of art for a specific purpose. (VA) • Begin to develop research skills. (L) • Decide on a purpose for reading and select material from a variety of sources. (L) • Create a media work. (L)	• Research rubric • Presentation of research done by creating a diorama
Role-play. Suggestion: Students develop a role-play in which one person is an interviewer from the year A.D. 3000. The interview will be played live on the Internet. The others in the group need to answer the interviewer's questions. Include the diorama in the interview.	• Demonstrate an understanding of voice and audience by speaking and writing in role as characters in a story. (D) • Demonstrate the ability to maintain concentration while in role. (D) • Explain the importance of research in producing effective dramatizations. (D)	• Teacher and peer evaluation • Rubrics: design and construction, research • Presentation rubric
Students summarize the learning experience by creating a "Then, Now, and Future" chart. They complete chart during a class discussion.	Describe the ways in which medieval society has influenced modern Western society. (SS)	Class and teacher evaluation

Source: Adrian DeTullio, Hamilton-Wentworth Catholic District School Board, Ontario, Canada; Debra Attenborough, Niagara Falls Art Gallery, Ontario, Canada; and Susan Drake.

Appendix B

Making Connections Template and Rubric

B-1: The Making Connections Template as Applied at East Bay High School

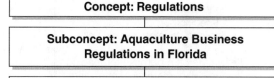

Concept: Regulations

Subconcept: Aquaculture Business Regulations in Florida

Cross-Curricular Standards

American Government

- The student understands the structure, functions, and purposes of government and how the principles and values of American democracy are reflected in American constitutional government.

- The student understands the nature of political authority and the nature of the relationship between government and civil society in limited governments (e.g., constitutional democracies)

Aquaculture Foundations

- The student applies scientific and technological principles to the aquacultural industry.

- The student describes the environmental requirements

Language Arts

Reading
- The student uses the reading process effectively.

- The student applies a variety of response strategies, including rereading, note taking, summarizing, outlining, writing a formal report, and relating what is read to his or her own experiences and feelings.

- The student constructs meaning from a wide range of texts.

(continued)

Lesson Title: Wimauma Woods vs. Steve T. Lapia

B-1: The Making Connections Template as Applied at East Bay High School (*continued*)

and unlimited governments (e.g., totalitarian regimes).

- The student understands the role of special-interest groups, political parties, the media, public opinion, and majority/minority conflicts on the development of public policy and the political process.

- The student understands the role of the citizens in American democracy.

- The student understands how personal, political, and economic rights are secured by constitutional government and by such means as the rule of law, checks and balances, an independent judiciary, and a vigilant citizenry.

necessary for a productive natural or man-made aquaculture system.

- The student understands the concept of best management practices (BMP) as applied to aquaculture.

- The student locates, gathers, analyzes, and evaluates written information for a variety of purposes, including research projects, real-world tasks, and self-improvement.

- The student selects and uses appropriate study and research skills and tools according to the type of information being gathered or organized, including almanacs, government publications, microfiche, news sources, and information services.

Writing
- The student uses writing processes effectively.

- The student writes to communicate ideas and information effectively.

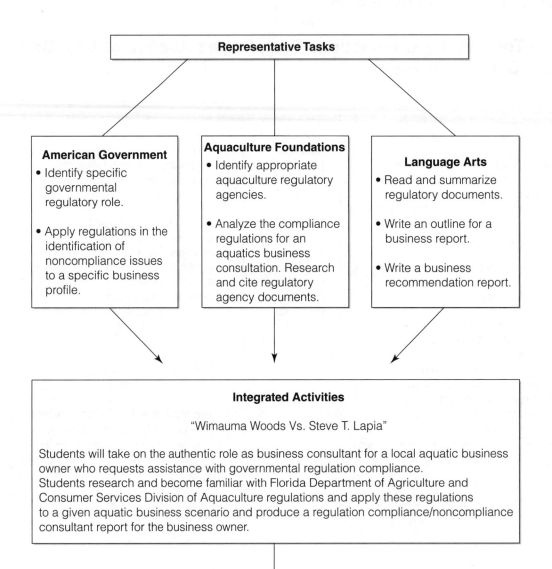

Representative Tasks

American Government
- Identify specific governmental regulatory role.

- Apply regulations in the identification of noncompliance issues to a specific business profile.

Aquaculture Foundations
- Identify appropriate aquaculture regulatory agencies.

- Analyze the compliance regulations for an aquatics business consultation. Research and cite regulatory agency documents.

Language Arts
- Read and summarize regulatory documents.

- Write an outline for a business report.

- Write a business recommendation report.

Integrated Activities

"Wimauma Woods Vs. Steve T. Lapia"

Students will take on the authentic role as business consultant for a local aquatic business owner who requests assistance with governmental regulation compliance.
Students research and become familiar with Florida Department of Agriculture and Consumer Services Division of Aquaculture regulations and apply these regulations to a given aquatic business scenario and produce a regulation compliance/noncompliance consultant report for the business owner.

Assessment
Consultant report evaluated by teachers using established rubric.

Source: Michael Yates, Charlotte Hughes, Sharon Morris, John Sporandio, and Diane Roberson, East Bay High School, Gibsonton, Florida.

B-2: A Making Connections Rubric from East Bay High School

Representative Task	Above Standard 4	At Standard 3	Below Standard 2	Not Met 0
Identify specific governmental regulatory roles.	Student identifies and understands the function of more than three federal, state, and local regulatory agencies.	Student identifies and understands the function of at least three regulatory agencies at each level of government: federal, state, and local.	Student identifies and understands the function of fewer than three regulatory agencies.	Student attempts to identify a few regulatory agencies.
Apply aquaculture-related regulations (identified in Aquaculture Foundations course) to identify noncompliance issues related in the profile.	Student identifies all appropriate regulations pertaining to all non-compliance issues described in the T. Lapia Farm Profile.	Student identifies most (60%) of the appropriate regulations pertaining to most of the non-compliance issues described in the profile.	Student identifies appropriate regulations pertaining to some (at least 50%) of the noncompliance issues described in the profile.	Student identifies regulations pertaining to a few of the non-compliance issues.
Identify appropriate aquaculture business regulatory agencies.	Student identifies and understands the function and role of all federal, state, and local regulatory agencies that regulate local aquaculture businesses.	Student identifies and understands the function and role of most federal, state, and local regulatory agencies that regulate local aquaculture businesses.	Student identifies some of the regulatory agencies that regulate local aqua-culture businesses.	Student identifies a few of the regulatory agencies that regulate local aqua-culture businesses.
Identify possible noncompliance issues based on the T. Lapia Farm Profile description.	Student identifies all noncompliance issues presented in the T. Lapia Farm Profile.	Student identifies most of the noncompliance issues.	Student identifies some of the noncompliance issues.	Student identifies a limited number (four or fewer) of the noncompliance issues.
Analyze and apply the compliance regulations.	Student creates an action plan for T. Lapia Farms citing all appropriate federal, state, and local regulations for all of the noncompliance issues and provides steps to be taken in order to reach compliance.	Student creates an action plan appropriately citing federal, state, and local regulations for most of the noncompliance issues and provides steps to be taken in order to reach compliance.	Student creates an action plan based on regulations for some of the noncom-pliance issues and provides steps to be taken in order to reach compliance.	Student creates an action plan for T. Lapia Farms based on regulations.

(continued)

B-2: A Making Connections Rubric from East Bay High School (continued)

Representative Task	Above Standard 4	At Standard 3	Below Standard 2	Not Met 0
Cite regulatory agency documents.	Student uses proper quotation, citation, and bibliography format to precisely cite regulatory documents.	Student uses proper citation format to cite regulatory documents.	Student correctly cites regulatory documents most of the time.	Student uses incorrect citation format.
Research, read, and summarize regulatory documents.	Student demonstrates ability to efficiently use research tools to locate regulations. Student is able to accurately summarize regulations based on careful reading.	Student demonstrates ability to use research tools. Student accurately summarizes regulations.	Student demonstrates use of research tools. Student summarizes regulations.	Student is not able to summarize regulations accurately.
Write an outline for a business report.	Student produces an organized outline for a written business report containing clearly identified noncompliance issues linked to cited and summarized regulations that must be met, as well as recommendations for actions to be taken to meet all compliance issues.	Student produces an organized outline for a written business report containing clearly identified noncompliance issues linked to regulations that must be met and a recommendation of steps to be taken to meet all compliance issues.	Student produces a poorly organized outline that does not clearly identify noncompliance issues linked to regulations. Recommendations exist but are not easy to follow.	Student produces an outline that has no coherent structure and does not resemble a business plan. There are no attempts at identifying noncompliance issues linked to regulations. No sound recommendations are made.
Write a business recommendation report.	Student produces an organized written business report containing clearly identified noncompliance issues linked to cited and summarized regulations that must be met, as well as recommendations for actions to be taken to meet all compliance issues.	Student produces an organized written business report containing identified noncompliance issues linked to regulations and a recommendation of steps to be taken to meet compliance issues.	Student produces a written business report that identifies a few noncompliance issues linked to regulations and offers a recommendation with only some of the steps to be taken to meet compliance issues.	Written business report is not organized and does not identify non-compliance issues or make suitable recommendations.

Source: Michael Yates, Charlotte Hughes, Sharon Morris, John Sporandio, and Diane Roberson, East Bay High School, Gibsonton, Florida.

Appendix C

Alpha Program Planning Sheet, Rubric, and Individualized Self-Assessment Criteria

C-1: Planning Sheet Used for Student-Generated Curriculum

They Came for Peace

The final theme of the 2002–2003 year is on movements of people that result in conflict or serenity. Students will explore a current event that has a major movement or settlement as part of its history.

Vermont Framework standards being assessed include the following:

- 6.8 Movements and Settlements: Students analyze the factors and implications associated with the historical and contemporary movements and settlements of people and groups in various times. (Locally and globally)

In addition students will work on their own individual Vital Results based on goals set with parents and teachers at 2nd trimester portfolio conferences.

Individual Expectations:

- Each student will select a Vermont writing genre. They will create a final piece of writing in this genre related to the movement they studied.

- Vocabulary.

- Read a book about the culture being studied or a major movement from some time in history.

(continued)

C-1: Planning Sheet Used for Student-Generated Curriculum
(*continued*)

- Complete the culminating event connection sheet. Students will be asked to find two movements that are similar to theirs and two movements that are significantly different from theirs.

Small-Group Expectations:

- Working in teams of four, students will explore a current event that is linked to a major movement or settlement. (Students select a partner, and then teachers place students into multiage, multi-gender groups of four.) Each group will create a critical question to guide their research. At the end of their research, students will present their responses to the critical question. This should address the following:

  - What impact did the movement have on the current event?

  - Why did the movement occur?

  - Was the movement forced or chosen, and what were common patterns based on that type of movement?

  - How did the incoming culture influence the existing culture (and vice versa)?

  - What systems affected or enabled this movement?

- Prepare a properly formatted bibliography with at least three to five different types of resources. Students should have one interview, e-mail response, or phone interview as a resource.

- Each group will trace their movement on an appropriate size-and-scope map.

Whole-Group Expectations:

- Create a large map of the world with different-colored strings marking each team's journey.

- Ask questions of a series of speakers from various cultures that have ended up in Vermont through a major movement or settlement.

- Participate in culminating event.

C-2: Student-Created Rubric

This rubric will allow us to assess how well each group has produced evidence toward meeting the standard for "They Came for Peace."

6.8. Movements and Settlements: Students analyze the factors and implications associated with the historical and contemporary movements and settlements of people and groups in various times. (Locally and globally)

	Exceeds Expectations	Meets Expectations	Nearly Meets Expectations	Needs Improvement
Critical Question and Research	Critical question is clearly articulated. The team has a properly formatted bibliography that demonstrates the use of at least three different types of resources. Has an interview or e-mail correspondence as part of research.	Critical question is clearly articulated. The team has a properly formatted bibliography that demonstrates the use of at least three different types of resources.	Critical question is clearly articulated. The team has a bibliography that demonstrates the use of at least two different types of resources.	Critical question is unclear. The team has no bibliography.
Visuals	Each member of the team has a visual component, all looking at different aspects of the critical question. Visuals are clear and interesting. Visuals are a complete answer to the critical question.	Each member of the team has a visual component, all looking at different aspects of the critical question. Visuals are clear and interesting.	Each member of the team has a visual component linked to the critical question. Visuals are somewhat clear and interesting.	Visuals are incomplete and are not of high quality.
Presentation	Each member is part of the presentation and can answer questions from the audience. Each member of the team has a complete understanding of their critical question and the team response to it. Excellent presentation skills.	Each member is part of the presentation and can answer questions from the audience. The team has a clear understanding of their critical question and the team response to it. Good presentation skills.	Each member is part of the presentation but cannot answer questions from the audience. The team has limited understanding of their critical question and the team response to it.	The team has little understanding of their critical question and the team response to it. Little evidence of teamwork.

C-3: Individual Self-Assessment Criteria Using Vermont's Vital Results

Name: _____   **Date:** _____

Alpha's Vital Results

Communication: I know I am developing my ability to communicate because I . . .

- Use a variety of strategies to read.
- Read grade-appropriate material.
- Read for meaning and demonstrate understanding through personal response.
- Comprehend and respond to a variety of media, images, and text.
- Draft, revise, edit, and critique written products.
- Respond to literature by showing understanding, making connections, and making judgments.
- Organize and convey information/ideas accurately in written reports.
- Organize and relate a series of events into a coherent procedure.
- Use persuasive writing to judge, propose, and persuade.
- Write effective personal essays.
- Listen actively and respond to communication.
- Critique what I hear.
- Use verbal and nonverbal skills to express myself effectively.
- Use a variety of forms (dance, music, theater, and visual arts) to create projects.
- Interpret and communicate using mathematical, scientific, and technological notation and representation.
- Use computers, telecommunications, and other tools.
- Use organizational systems to obtain information.
- Use graphs, charts, and other visual presentations to communicate.
- Select appropriate technologies and applications to solve problems.

Functioning Independently: As a part of my continuing development as an independent learner I . . .

- Assume responsibility for my own learning by setting and assessing goals.
- Identify priorities and budget my time.
- Meet deadlines.
- Follow through on commitments.
- Know how, when, and where to ask for help.
- Initiate, plan, carry out, present, and assess an independent project.
- Recognize both my successes and failures as opportunities for new learning.

Personal Development: As I continue to strengthen a unique sense of self-worth and personal competence, I . . .

- Assess my own learning by developing rigorous criteria for myself and use these to produce consistently high-quality work.
- Assess how I learn best and use additional supplemental strategies.
- Demonstrate respect for myself and others.
- Understand intellectual, physical, social, and emotional stages of my development.
- Exercise regularly and demonstrate competence/proficiency.

(*continued*)

C-3: Individual Self-Assessment Criteria Using Vermont's Vital Results (*continued*)

- Make informed decisions.
- Demonstrate an understanding of personal economic decisions.
- Perform effectively on teams.
- Interact respectfully with others.
- Use systematic and collaborative problem-solving strategies.
- Analyze my roles and responsibilities.
- Demonstrate dependability, productivity, and initiative.
- Know about various careers.
- Develop a plan about current and continued education and training.

Reasoning and Problem Solving: I am growing confident in my reasoning and problem-solving abilities because I . . .

- Ask a variety of questions.
- Use reasoning strategies, knowledge, and common sense to solve problems.
- Devise and test ways of improving the effectiveness of a system.
- Produce solutions to mathematical problems requiring decisions about approach and presentation.
- Apply prior knowledge, curiosity, imagination, and creativity to solve problems.
- Respond to new information by reflecting on experience and reconsidering my opinion and sources of information.
- Demonstrate a willingness to take risks in order to learn.
- Persevere in the face of challenges and obstacles.
- Design a product, project, or service to meet an identified need.
- Plan and organize an activity.

Civic and Social Responsibility: As I continue to develop my civic and social responsibilities, I . . .

- Take an active and positive role in the community.
- Participate actively in the democratic process.
- Respect and value human diversity.
- Understand the concept of prejudice and its effects on various groups.
- Understand both continuity and change.
- Respect all forms of life and take steps to protect and repair the environment.

Source: Vermont Department of Education, 1996.

Additional Resources

Curriculum integration involves every aspect of curriculum design, from a philosophical perspective to alignment of standards, assessment, and instructional strategies. We believe the following resources are useful for those seeking to integrate curriculum, though the list is by no means exhaustive.

Understanding by Design: Designing Backward

Wiggins, G., & McTighe, J. (1998). *Understanding by design.* Alexandria, VA: Association for Supervision and Curriculum Development.

To integrate the curriculum and cover standards, teachers need to use a backward design approach. This approach is the core of the Understanding by Design (UbD) series, which is extensive and well worth investigating. Whether you wish to access the series in whole or in part (such as through a three-videotape set), products related to it are available on the Web site of the Association for Supervision and Curriculum Development (ASCD, http://www.ascd.org).

Curriculum Mapping

Jacobs, H. H. (1997). *Mapping the big picture: Integrating curriculum and assessment.* Alexandria, VA: Association for Supervision and Curriculum Development.

This is an easy-to-read book on how to map the curriculum for the school year—the first step for integrating the curriculum. Jacobs believes that each teacher should map the curriculum. When viewing all curriculum maps, they are then able to see the big picture of curriculum for the school and identify gaps and unintended curricular repetitions as well as potential areas for curriculum integration.

———

Burns, R. (2001). Curriculum mapping: Curriculum renewal. In ASCD's *Curriculum Handbook.* Alexandria, VA: Association for Supervision and Curriculum Development.

In this book, Rebecca adds a standards-based perspective to curriculum mapping. She offers examples of how five school districts used curriculum mapping to achieve alignment with state standards and increase student performance on standardized tests.

Integrated Curriculum

The books highlighted here focus on curriculum integration in general rather than on integrating any specific subject across the curriculum. These books are standards-based unless otherwise noted.

Alvardo, A., & Herr, P. (2003). *Inquiry-based learning using everyday objects: Hands-on instructional strategies that promote active learning in grades 3–8.* Thousand Oaks, CA: Corwin Press.

This unusual and interesting book focuses on using everyday objects as the organizing center of a lesson. Most lessons begin from a science base and then extend to connect to other subject areas. The authors emphasize the interdisciplinary skill of categorization and provide sample lesson plans with suggested formats for formative and summative evaluation.

———

Burns, R. (1995, 1999). *Dissolving the boundaries: Planning for curriculum integration in middle and secondary schools.* Charleston, WV: Appalachia Educational Laboratory. (Available from Scarecrow Publishing Company.)

Middle and high school faculties will find this book useful as they make decisions regarding curriculum integration. Teachers may use the book effectively in groups to gain a better understanding of curriculum integration, assess their readiness to begin integrating curriculum, and prepare for the interdisciplinary team approach. A Facilitator's Guide with professional development activities is also available.

Drake, S. M. (2000). Integrated curriculum. In ASCD's *Curriculum Handbook*. Alexandria, VA: Association for Supervision and Curriculum Development.

This chapter in ASCD's *Curriculum Handbook* series offers many of the same concepts as this book along with other examples of rigorous and relevant curriculum implemented in schools across North America. It also includes a section on problem-based learning.

————

Drake, S. M. (1998). *Creating integrated curriculum: Proven ways to increase student learning*. Thousand Oaks, CA: Corwin Press.

This book features a collection of the most popular integration models to have emerged in the early 90s, including work by Jacobs, Fogarty, Erickson, Beane, Lauritzen, Jaeger, and Harris and Carr. Each model is fully developed and accompanied by a description of its essential ideas and a teacher-created example. Though standards are discussed in detail, the reader will need to make the connections to standards for some of the models, as they are not standards-based.

————

Erickson, H. L. (2001). *Stirring the head, heart, and soul: Redefining curriculum and instruction* (2nd ed.). Thousand Oaks, CA: Corwin Press.

To gain a deep understanding of concept-based education, educators should read this book. It is most informative, rich in both theory and practice, and presents detailed sample standards-based units developed in real school districts at all grade levels. The book covers all the essentials that educators need to know to develop rigorous and relevant curriculum.

————

Fogarty, R. (1997). *Problem-based learning and other curriculum models for the multiple intelligences classroom*. Arlington Heights, IL: Skylight.

This book features six models: problem-based learning, case studies, thematic learning, project learning, service learning, and performance learning. Each framework is presented in an easy-to-read format and applies to grades K–12. Although only one model is about curriculum integration, the others do have interdisciplinary applications. The innovations in this book are not standards-based, but the book is full of good ideas that could be adapted to standards-based units.

————

Jacobs, H. H. (Ed.) (1989). *Interdisciplinary curriculum: Design and implementation*. Alexandria, VA: Association for Supervision and Curriculum Development.

This book is a classic that has stood the test of time. Jacobs offers a rationale for interdisciplinary work and criteria to ensure rigor, describes two interdisciplinary programs in detail, and presents a step-by-step approach (key points of which include guiding questions and using Bloom's taxonomy as an organizer). Though written before the days of backward design and standards, her template can be adapted to today's context. The book also includes an interesting chapter by David Perkins on selecting a substantive theme. His chapter fits well within the context of concept-based education.

Martin-Kniep, G. O. (2000). *Becoming a better teacher.* Alexandria, VA: Association for Supervision and Curriculum Development.

This excellent book outlines eight innovations that work in student-centered classrooms, including integrated curriculum, essential questions, standards-based curriculum and assessment design, authentic assessment, scoring rubrics, portfolios, reflection, and action research. Although curriculum integration is the focus of only one chapter in the book, the other chapters describe important ingredients for successful integration.

Meinback, A. M., Fredericks, A., & Rothlein, L. (2000). *The complete guide to thematic units* (2nd ed). Norwood, MA: Christopher Gordon.

This book is filled with rich examples of primary and intermediate thematic curriculum. It offers general tips for planning and implementing thematic units, including chapters on authentic assessment and parent and community involvement. Nine units for primary and 10 units for intermediate grades are fully developed; each unit includes literature-related activities. There are many great ideas in this book to inspire the reader, and it would be relatively easy to adapt the units so that they are standards-based.

Mitchell, R., Willis, M., & Chicago Teachers Union Quest Center. (1995). *Learning in overdrive: Designing curriculum, instruction, and assessment from standards.* Golden, CO: North American Press.

This book was ahead of its time. It takes a backward design approach to standards and offers a step-by-step template to designing integrated curriculum; in addition, it uses a process very similar to the scan-and-cluster approach discussed in this book. Written in a conversational style, this is an excellent guide for educators wishing to design curriculum that fits accountability mandates.

Ronis, D. (2002). *Clustering standards in integrated units.* Arlington Heights, IL: Skylight Professional Development.

This book operates from the same premise as our book: that teachers can plan lessons that are engaging and cover the standards. Attractively formatted, it offers large graphics that are easy to understand quickly. The book also includes a template for designing integrated units and a number of fully developed sample units using the template, which includes a culminating task organizer, unit planning map, interdisciplinary lesson plan, culminating task rubric, unit overview, and rubrics. The national content area standards are used in the samples. Though we like the title and simplicity of presentation in this book, there is a lot missing; for example, there is no direction on how to cluster the standards in integrated units.

———

Wilkinson, P., McNutt, M. A., & Friedan, E. (2003). *Practical teaching methods K to 6: Sparking the flame of learning.* Thousand Oaks, CA: Corwin.

This book is written by and for educators. The authors have a wealth of experience, and they offer many practical instructional tools that work. They address the traditional subject areas and include technology and the library media center, and make a point of addressing cross-disciplinary connections in each subject area. The authors use the national standards as the framework for each content area.

Klein, J. T. (Ed.) 2002. *Interdisciplinary education in K–12 and college: A foundation for K–16 dialogue.* New York: The College Board.

This unique book informs educators on both sides of the school-college divide. Eight specialists in interdisciplinary education engage in a stimulating dialogue about the curricular visions that characterize K–12 and K–16. They discuss questions ranging from the use of technology in teaching, team teaching, and integrative processes and conceptions to political stakes, pedagogy, and program management. Rebecca wrote a chapter on interdisciplinary teamed instruction for this volume.

Videos

We know that many videos are very valuable learning tools, but they also tend to be too expensive for an individual to purchase. We recommend that you look at the resources in the district office and use what is available. The following videos are particularly useful for developing relevant and rigorous curriculum.

Jacobs, H. H. (1999). *Curriculum mapping: Charting the course for content.* Alexandria, VA: Association for Supervision and Curriculum Development. (This video offers steps to map the curriculum.)

Erickson, H. L. (1997). *Planning integrated units: A concept-based approach*. Alexandria, VA: Association for Supervision and Curriculum Development. (This video offers a good explanation of concept-based education and how it applies to curriculum integration.)

———

Erickson, H. L. (2002). *Creating concept-based curriculum for deeper understanding*. Thousand Oaks, CA: Corwin Press. (This video offers more insights into concept-based education.)

Newsletters

The GLEF Blast Newsletter.

The newsletter of the George Lucas Educational Foundation (GLEF) features schools across the United States that are involved in innovative projects. Most of the examples feature interdisciplinary curriculum and integrate technology into the curriculum. This bi-monthly e-newsletter delivers news, research, and inspiring stories from the frontlines of K–12 education. To subscribe, send an e-mail to e-newsletter@glef.org.

References

Aikin, W. M. (1942). *The story of the eight-year study.* New York: Harper.

Albright, J. J., Purohit, K. D., & Walsh, C. S. (2001). *Building a curriculum of critical multiliteracies in interdisciplinary classrooms through collaborative research.* Paper presented at the meeting of the Canadian Society for Studies in Education, Quebec City, PQ, Canada.

Allen, R. (2003). The democratic aim of service learning. *Educational Leadership, 60*(6), 51–54.

Association for Supervision and Curriculum Development. (1997). *Planning integrated units: A concept-based approach* [Video]. Alexandria, VA: Author.

Barry, J. (2001). On course to higher test scores: Prof's methods receiving credit. *Miami Herald.* Avaliable: http://www.herald.com/content/today/news.dade/digdoes/106960.htm

Beane, J. (1990/1993). *A middle school curriculum: From rhetoric to reality.* Columbus, OH: National Middle School Association.

Beane, J. (1997). *Curriculum integration: Designing the core of democratic education.* New York: Teachers College Press.

Blake, B. (2001). New program will put artists in Asheville and Buncombe schools to support academic curriculum. Citizen-Times.com. Available: http://www.citizen-times.com /cgi-bin/story.cgi?news&20010129_nl.txt.

Bloom, B. S. (1956). *A taxonomy of educational objectives* (Handbook 1, Cognitive domain). New York: McKay.

Brazee, E., & Capelluti, J. (1994). The middle level curriculum: Getting where we need to be! *The Journal of the New England League of Middle Schools, 7*(1), 1–6.

Brophy, J. (2000). *Teaching* (Educational Practices Series Booklet No. 1). Brussels, Belgium: International Academy of Education. Reprinted by Laboratory for Student Success, Philadelphia, PA.

Brown, D. F. (2002, September). Self-directed learning in an 8th grade class. *Educational Leadership, 60*(1), 54–58.

Burns, R. (1995). *Dissolving the boundaries: Planning for curriculum integration in middle and secondary schools* from http://www.ael.org. Charleston, WV: Appalachia Educational Laboratory.

Burns, R. (2001). Curriculum renewal: Curriculum mapping. A chapter in the *Curriculum Handbook*. Alexandria, VA: Association for Supervision and Curriculum Development.

Caine, R., & Caine, G. (1991). *Making connections: Teaching and the human brain*. Alexandria, VA: Association for Supervision and Curriculum Development.

Caine, R., & Caine, G. (1997). *Education on the edge of possibility*. Alexandria, VA: Association for Supervision and Curriculum Development.

Case, R. (1994). Our crude handling of educational reform: The case of curricular integration. *Canadian Journal of Education, 19*(1), 80–93.

Chard, S. (1998). *The project approach*. New York: Scholastic.

Clark, B. (1988). *Growing up gifted* (3rd ed.). Toronto, Canada: Merrill.

Corwin Press. (2002). *Creating concept-based curriculum for deeper understanding* [Video kit]. Thousand Oaks, CA: Author.

Covey, S. (1990). *Seven habits of highly effective people*. New York: Simon & Schuster.

Creating caring schools. (2003, March). *Educational Leadership, 60*(6).

Curtis, D. (2002, September). The power of projects. *Educational Leadership, 60*(1), 50–53.

Curtis, D. (2003). A+ for empathy. *Edutopia*. Available: http://glef.org/empathy.html.

Daquilante, R. (2002). Driving instruction with data. A presentation to Kanawha County principals, Charleston, WV.

DeRoche, E. F., & Williams, M. M. (2001). *Educating hearts and minds: A comprehensive character education framework* (2nd ed.). Thousand Oaks, CA: Corwin.

Drake, S. M. (1991, October). How our team dissolved the boundaries. *Educational Leadership, 49*(2), 20–22.

Drake, S. M. (1993). *Planning integrated curriculum: The call to adventure*. Alexandria, VA: Association for Supervision and Curriculum Development.

Drake, S. M. (1995). Connecting learning outcomes to integrated curriculum. *Orbit, 26*(1), 28–32.

Drake, S. M. (1998). *Creating integrated curriculum: Proven ways to increase student learning*. Thousand Oaks, CA: Corwin.

Drake, S. M. (2000). Integrated curriculum. A chapter in the *Curriculum Handbook*. Alexandria, VA: Association for Supervision and Curriculum Development.

Drake, S. M. (2001, September). Castles, kings . . . and standards. *Educational Leadership, 59*(1), 38–42.

Elmore, R. F., & Rothman, R. (1999). *Testing, teaching, and learning: A guide for states and school districts*. Washington, DC: National Academy Press.

English, F. W. (1980, April). Curriculum mapping. *Educational Leadership, 37*(7), 558–559.

Erickson, H. L. (1998). *Concept-based curriculum and instruction: Teaching beyond the facts*. Thousand Oaks, CA: Corwin.

Erickson, H. L. (2001). *Stirring the head, heart, and soul: Refining curriculum and instruction* (2nd ed.). Thousand Oaks, CA: Corwin.

Erlandson, C., & McVittie, J. (2001). Student voices on integrative curriculum. *Middle School Journal, 33*(2), 28–36.

Expeditionary Learning Outward Bound. (2001). Evidence of success. Available: http://www.elob.org/evidence/evidence.html.

Findley, N. (2002, September). In their own ways. *Educational Leadership, 60*(1), 60–63.

Fiske, E. E. (1999). Champions of change: The impact of the arts on learning. Available: http://www.aep-arts.org/Champions.html.

Fogarty, R. (1991). *The mindful school: How to integrate the curricula*. Palatine, IL: Skylight.

Furger, R. (2001). Laptops for all. The George Lucas Educational Foundation. Available: http://glef.org/

GLEF Staff. (2001). Project-based learning research. Available: http://glef.org/

Glenn, J. (2001). The benefits of service learning. *Harvard Education Letter Research Online*. Available: http://www.edletter.org/current/glenn.shtml

Gordon, D. T. (2002). Moving instruction to center stage. *Harvard Education Letter Research Online*. Available: http://www.edletter.org/current/index.shtml

Grossman, P., Wineburg, S., & Beers, S. (2000). Introduction: When theory meets practice in the world of school. In S. Wineburg and P. Grossman (Eds.), *Interdisciplinary curriculum: Challenges to implementation* (pp. 1–16). New York: Teachers College Press.

Guskey, T. R. (2003, February). How classroom assessments improve learning. *Educational Leadership, 60*(5), 7–11.

Hargreaves, A. (2001). Beyond subjects and standards: A critical view of educational reform. *Ontario ASCD*, 46–51.

Hargreaves, A., & Moore, S. (2000). Curriculum integration and classroom relevance: A study of teachers' practice. *Journal of Curriculum and Supervision, 15*(2), 89–112.

Hartzler, D. H. (2000). *A meta-analysis of studies conducted on integrated curriculum programs and their effects on student achievement*. Unpublished Ed.D. dissertation, Indiana University, Bloomington.

Horwood, B. (2002). The influence of outdoor education on curriculum integration: A case study. *Pathways, 14*(4), 6–12.

Inlay, L. (2003, March). Values: The implicit curriculum. *Educational Leadership, 60*(6), 69–71.

Jacobs, H. H. (Ed.). (1989). *Interdisciplinary curriculum: Design and implementation.* Alexandria, VA: Association for Supervision and Curriculum Development.

Jacobs, H. H. (1997). *Mapping the big picture: Integrating curriculum and assessment, K–12.* Alexandria, VA: Association for Supervision and Curriculum Development.

Jensen, E. (1998). *Teaching with the brain in mind.* Alexandria, VA: Association for Supervision and Curriculum Development.

Jervis, C., Bull, S., Sauter, G., & Turner, P. (1998). Making connections: Interdisciplinary teamed instruction as a tool for change. Appalachia Educational Laboratory. Available: http://www.ael.org/link/v17n4/dissolve.htm

Kessler, R. (2000). *The soul of education.* Alexandria, VA: Association for Supervision and Curriculum Development.

Klein, J. T. (Ed.). (2002). *Interdisciplinary education in K–12 and college: A foundation for K–16 dialogue.* New York: College Board.

Lang, M. (2003, April). *Global perspectives on integrated curriculum.* Paper presented at the annual meeting of the American Educational Research Association, Chicago, IL.

Levy, S. (1996). *Starting from scratch: One classroom builds its own curriculum.* Portsmouth, NH: Heinemann.

Martin-Kniep, G. O., Fiege, D. M., & Soodak, L. C. (1995). Curriculum integration: An expanded view of an abused idea. *Journal of Curriculum and Supervision, 10*(3), 227–249.

Maurer, R. E. (1994). *Designing interdisciplinary curriculum in middle, junior, and high school.* Needham Heights, MA: Allyn & Bacon.

Miller, J. P., Cassie, B., & Drake, S. M. (1990). *Holistic learning: A teacher's guide to integrated studies.* Toronto, Canada: OISE Press.

Mitchell, F. M. (1998). *The effects of curriculum alignment on mathematics achievement of third-grade students as measured by the Iowa Test of Basic Skills: Implications for educational administrators.* Unpublished dissertation, Clark Atlanta University, Atlanta, GA.

Muir, M. (2001). What engages underachieving middle school students in learning? *Middle School Journal, 33*(2), 37–43.

Murphy, M. O., & Singer, A. J. (2001). Asking the big questions: Teaching about the great Irish famine and world history. *Social Education, 65*(5), 286–291.

National Council of Teachers of English. (1935). *An experience curriculum in English.* New York: D. Appleton-Century.

National Council of Teachers of Mathematics. (2000). *Principles and standards for school mathematics.* Reston, VA: Author.

National Middle School Association. (2002). NMSA position statement on curriculum integration [online]. Available: http://www.nmsa.org/news/positionpapers/integrativecurriculum.htm

Ontario Ministry of Education. (1998). *The Ontario Curriculum Grades 9 and 10 Mathematics.* Toronto, Canada: Queen's Printer for Ontario. Available: http://www.edu.gov.on.ca

Ontario Ministry of Education. (1999). *The Ontario Curriculum Grades 9 and 10 English.* Toronto, Canada: Queen's Printer for Ontario. Available: http://www.edu.gov.on.ca

Ontario Ministry of Education. (2000). *The Ontario Curriculum Grades 11 and 12 English.* Toronto, Canada: Queen's Printer for Ontario. Available: http://www.edu.gov.on.ca

Ontario Ministry of Education. (2000). *The Ontario Curriculum Grades 11 and 12 Health and Physical Education.* Toronto, Canada: Queen's Printer for Ontario. Available: http://www.edu.gov.on.ca

Ontario Ministry of Education. (2000). *The Ontario Curriculum Grades 11 and 12 Mathematics.* Toronto, Canada: Queen's Printer for Ontario. Available: http://www.edu.gov.on.ca

Ontario Ministry of Education. (2000). *The Ontario Curriculum Grades 11 and 12 Science.* Toronto, Canada: Queen's Printer for Ontario. Available: at http://www.edu.gov.on.ca

Ontario Ministry of Education. (2000). *The Ontario Curriculum Grades 11 and 12 Social Sciences and Humanities.* Toronto, Canada: Queen's Printer for Ontario. Available at http://www.edu.gov.on.ca

Ontario Ministry of Education. (2000). *The Ontario Curriculum Grades 11 and 12 The Arts.* Toronto, Canada: Queen's Printer for Ontario. Available: http://www.edu.gov.on.ca

Ontario Ministry of Education. (2002). *The Ontario Curriculum Grades 11 and 12 Interdisciplinary Studies.* Toronto, Canada: Queen's Printer for Ontario. Available: http://www.edu.gov.on.ca

Ontario Ministry of Education and Training. (1997). *The Ontario Curriculum Grades 1–8 Language.* Toronto, Canada: Queen's Printer for Ontario. Available: http://www.edu.gov.on.ca

Ontario Ministry of Education and Training. (1997). *The Ontario Curriculum Grades 1–8 Mathematics.* Toronto, Canada: Queen's Printer for Ontario. Available at http://www.edu.gov.on.ca

Ontario Ministry of Education and Training. (1998). *The Ontario Curriculum Grades 1–8 Science and Technology.* Toronto, Canada: Queen's Printer for Ontario. Available: http://www.edu.gov.on.ca

Ontario Ministry of Education and Training. (1998). *The Ontario Curriculum Grades 1–8 The Arts.* Toronto, Canada: Queen's Printer for Ontario. Available: http://www.edu.gov.on.ca

Ontario Ministry of Education and Training. (1998). *The Ontario Curriculum Social Studies Grades 1 to 6 History and Geography Grades 7 and 8.* Toronto, Canada: Queen's Printer for Ontario. Available: http://www.edu.gov.on.ca

Ontario Ministry of Education and Training. (1999). *The Ontario Curriculum Grades 9 and 10 Health and Physical Education.* Toronto, Canada: Queen's Printer for Ontario. Available: http://www.edu.gov.on.ca

Ontario Ministry of Education and Training. (1999). *The Ontario Curriculum Grades 9 and 10 Science and Technology.* Toronto, Canada: Queen's Printer for Ontario. Available: http://www.edu.gov.on.ca

Ontario Ministry of Education and Training. (1999). *The Ontario Curriculum Grades 9 and 10 Social Sciences and the Humanities.* Toronto, Canada: Queen's Printer for Ontario. Available: http://www.edu.gov.on.ca

Patten, S. (2001). Literacy development through curriculum integration. *Ontario ASCD,* 63–64.

Québec Education Program: New directions for success (Preschool Education, Elementary Education). (2001). Québec, Canada: Education Ministry of Québec.

Ragland, J. (2002). Kids project learning into the community. Latimes.com. Available: http://www.latimes.com/la-000018344mar13.story

Reading and writing in the content areas. (2002, November). *Educational Leadership, 60*(3).

Secretary's Commission on Achieving Necessary Skills. (1991). *What work requires of schools: A SCANS report for America 2000.* Washington, DC: U.S. Department of Labor, Secretary's Commission on Achieving Necessary Skills.

Smith, C., & Myers, C. (2001). Students take center stage in classroom assessment. *Middle Ground, 5*(2), 10–16.

Smith, G. A. (2002, September). Going local. *Educational Leadership, 60*(1), 30–33.

Stevenson, C., & Carr, J. (Eds.). (1993). *Integrated studies in the middle grades: Dancing through walls.* New York: Teachers College Press.

Taba, H. (1966). *Teaching strategies and cognitive functioning in elementary school* [Cooperative research project]. Washington, DC: Office of Education, U.S. Department of Health, Education, and Welfare.

Thomas-Lester, A. (2001). Peace is guiding force at Mt. Rainier Elementary. Washington Post Online. Available: http://www.washingtonpost.com/ac2/wp-dyn?pagename=article&node=&contentId=A61180-2001Oct2

Tolbert, K. (2001). For Japanese students, less may be more. *Washington Post* Online. Available: http://www.washingtonpost.com/wp-dyn/articles/A55926-2001oct1.html

Tomlinson, C. A., Kaplan, S. N., Renzulli, J. S., Purcell, J., Leppien, J., & Burns, D. (2002). *The parallel curriculum: A design to develop high potential and challenge high-ability learners.* Thousand Oaks, CA: Corwin.

Topping, D. H., & McManus, R. A. (2002, November). A culture of literacy in science. *Educational Leadership, 60*(3), 30–33.

Upitis, R., & Smithirin, K. (2002). *Learning Through the Arts™ national assessment 1999–2002 final report to the Royal Conservatory of Music.* Available: http://www.ltta.ca

Vars, G. F. (2000). Editorial comment: On research, high stakes testing, and core philosophy. *The Core Teacher, 50*(1), 3.

Vars, G. F. (2001a). Can curriculum integration survive in an era of high-stakes testing? *Middle School Journal, 33*(2), 7–17.

Vars, G. F. (2001b). Signatures for students' position statement question standards movement. *The Core Teacher, 51*(1), 1.

Venville, G., Wallace, J., Rennie, L., & Malone, J. (1999). *Science, mathematics, and technology case studies of integrated curriculum.* Perth, Australia: Education Department of Western Australia.

Vermont Department of Education. (1996). *Vermont framework of standards and learning opportunities.* Montpelier, VT: Author.

Wang, L., & Su, L. (2002, April). *Curriculum reform of science education in Chinese primary and secondary schools.* Paper presented at the annual conference of the National Association for Research in Science Teaching, New Orleans, LA.

Warner, E., & Heinz, M. (2002). *Report on the action research findings: How the DaimlerChrysler-Michigan Department of Education teams implemented the Making Connections Curriculum Integration Project.* Rohnert Park, CA: Sonoma State University.

Weilbacher, G. (2001). Is curriculum integration an endangered species? *Middle School Journal, 33*(2), 18–27.

Weissberg, R. P., Resnik, H., Payton, J., & O'Brien, M. U. (2003). Evaluating social and emotional learning programs. *Educational Leadership, 60*(6), 46–50.

Wiggins, G., & McTighe, J. (1998). *Understanding by design.* Alexandria, VA: Association for Supervision and Curriculum Development.

Wilgoren, J. (2001). In a society of their own, children are learning. *New York Times* on the Web. Available: http://www.nytimes.com/2001/02/07/nyregion/07MICR

Wineburg, S., & Grossman, P. (2000). *Interdisciplinary curriculum: Challenges to implementation*. New York: Teachers College Press.

Wishnick, T. K. (1989). Relative effects on achievement scores of SES, gender, teacher effect, and instructional alignment. A study of alignment's power in mastery learning. *Dissertation Abstracts International, 51*(04A), 1107 (University Microfilms No. 9019604).

Wraga, W. (1996). A century of interdisciplinary curriculum in American schools. In W. Wraga (Ed.), *Annual review of research for school leaders* (pp. 118–145). New York: Scholastic.

Wraga, W. (1997). Patterns of interdisciplinary curriculum organization and professional knowledge of the curriculum field. *Journal of Curriculum and Supervision, 12*(2), 98–117.

Index

Page references for figures are followed by *f*, as in 35*f*.

About the Authors

Susan M. Drake is a professor at the Faculty of Education, Brock University, St. Catharines, Ontario. She holds a doctorate in curriculum from the University of Toronto. Susan has had an extensive career teaching in classrooms from primary grades through higher education. She has been actively involved in designing and implementing integrated approaches to curriculum both at the provincial and state level and in the classroom. Currently she teaches courses on interdisciplinary curriculum for students working toward graduate education degrees. This is her sixth book on integrated curriculum; other books include *Planning Integrated Curriculum: The Call to Adventure* (1993) and *Creating Integrated Curriculum: Proven Ways to Increase Student Learning* (1998). Susan has acted as a consultant and has delivered workshops across North America and internationally. She can be reached by e-mail at sdrake@ed.brocku.ca or by phone at 905-688-5550, ext. 3931.

Rebecca C. Burns is a senior research and development specialist at Appalachia Educational Laboratory (AEL) in Charleston, West Virginia. She holds a masters degree in speech from Marshall University, and she has completed postgraduate work in curriculum design and supervision. The findings from her two-year study of curriculum integration in four Virginia schools led to formation of the Interdisciplinary Teamed Instruction professional development program at AEL. Rebecca has conducted graduate courses, institutes, and workshops on curriculum integration and curriculum mapping for educators across the United States and in Puerto Rico. She is the author of *Dissolving the Boundaries: Planning for Curriculum Integration in Middle and Secondary Schools* (2001), and has written a book-length chapter on curriculum mapping in ASCD's *Curriculum Handbook* (2001) and a chapter for the College Board's edited volume, *Interdisciplinary Education in K–12 and College* (2002). Rebecca is a former teacher of middle school through graduate levels. She may be contacted by e-mail at burnsr@ael.org or by phone at 304-347-0472.

Related ASCD Resources

At the time of publication, the following ASCD resources were available; for the most up-to-date information about ASCD resources, go to www.ascd.org. ASCD stock numbers are noted in parentheses.

Audiotapes

Working Smarter in Curriculum Design by Grant Wiggins and Jay McTighe (#201114S25)

Curriculum Mapping: A Tool for Instructional Decision Making by Chris Stewart (#203080S25)

Standards and Interdisciplinary Curriculum: Using Meaningful Connections to Support the Standards by Roxann Rose (#202091S25)

Books

Integrated Curriculum: Design and Implementation edited by Heidi Hayes Jacobs (#61189156)

A Comprehensive Guide to Designing Standards-Based Districts, Schools, and Classrooms by Robert J. Marzano and John S. Kendall (#196215)

Succeeding with Standards: Linking Curriculum, Assessment, and Action Planning by Judy F. Carr and Douglas E. Harris (#101005)

Multimedia

Curriculum Integration Professional Inquiry Kit by Carol Cummings (#998214S25)

Implementing Standards-Based Education Inquiry Kit by Jane Ellison and Carolee Hayes (#999222S25)

Videos

Raising Achievement Through Standards (3 tapes with facilitator's guide, #498043S25)

Integrating the Curriculum by Heidi Hayes Jacobs (2 tapes, #614248S25)